Mapping the Way from Teacher Preparation to edTPA® Completion

Mapping the Way from Teacher Preparation to edTPA® Completion

A Guide for Secondary Education Candidates

Jason C. Fitzgerald and Michelle L. Schpakow

Rutgers University Press

New Brunswick, Camden, and Newark, New Jersey, and London

Library of Congress Cataloging-in-Publication Data
Names: Fitzgerald, Jason C., author. | Schpakow, Michelle L., author.
Title: Mapping the way from teacher preparation to edTPA completion : a guide for
secondary education candidates / Jason C. Fitzgerald, Michelle L. Schpakow.
Description: New Brunswick : Rutgers University Press, [2021] |
Includes bibliographical references and index.
Identifiers: LCCN 2020041774 | ISBN 9781978821989 (hardcover) |
ISBN 9781978821972 (paperback) | ISBN 9781978821996 (epub) |
ISBN 9781978822009 (mobi) | ISBN 9781978822016 (pdf)
Subjects: LCSH: Portfolios in education—United States. | Employment portfolios—
United States. | Student teachers—Rating of—United States. | High school teachers—
Certification—United States. | High school teachers—Training of—United States.
Classification: LCC LB1728 .F57 2021 | DDC 370.71/1—dc23
LC record available at https://lccn.loc.gov/2020041774

A British Cataloging-in-Publication record for this book is available
from the British Library.

∞ The paper used in this publication meets the requirements of the
American National Standard for Information Sciences—
Permanence of Paper for Printed Library Materials,
ANSI Z39.48-1992.

www.rutgersuniversitypress.org

Manufactured in the United States of America

Contents

Mapping the Way from Teacher Preparation to
edTPA® Completion

Introduction

Mapping the Way from Teacher Preparation to edTPA Completion: A Guide for Secondary Education Candidates is a resource to use as you prepare your edTPA portfolio. In our experience, teacher candidates (and sometimes teacher educators) can fail to see the connections edTPA makes to sound teaching practices. The purpose of this book is to highlight these areas, demonstrating to you *how* the theories and strategies you learned throughout your teacher preparation coursework apply to the edTPA expectations for a successful teaching portfolio. We hope to help you recognize that the edTPA is not asking you to do things that are different from, or in addition to, your traditional planning, instruction, and assessment practices during student teaching. Recognizing the overlap between teacher preparation coursework, student teaching practice, and edTPA expectations will help you to better develop, and better explain, your instructional decisions within your edTPA portfolio.

Lost with Directions: An Analogy

In our GPS-dependent world, human beings increasingly rely on step-by-step directions to get them from Point A to Point B.

Even when people know where they are going, they are still known to use their GPS-enabled devices to find the fastest route—even if it is only the fastest by less than a minute. There is a security in following those directions, especially when they are paired with warning signals. Even when you are by yourself driving to somewhere vaguely familiar, it is nice to know that you have a metaphorical "extra pair of eyes" watching street signs, telling you where to turn, where the police are setting speed traps, and when there is traffic ahead. Indeed, such crowd-source-enhanced step-by-step directions make travel much easier—until they don't.

We have all heard stories of step-by-step directions gone wrong. Driving in Croatia with my wife, I (Jason) followed the GPS up the A-1 from Dubrovnik to Split. The GPS navigation provided a good deal of comfort, especially driving in another country. Not only was I sure that I was heading in the correct direction, but I was also alerted to speed changes, sharp turns, and traffic patterns, especially as we exited Dubrovnik and entered Split. The navigation system even estimated our time to our next Airbnb apartment so that we could alert our host when we were close to our destination.

The navigation was precise, which was immensely helpful as we headed into Split, a city that seemed to lack any ninety-degree street corners. The streets were crowded with people and cars; the GPS allowed us to navigate to the correct streets. Following the GPS, though, I failed to realize that the streets were getting narrower and narrower. Cars still lined the streets on both sides, but they looked different from the sedan I was driving; they were much smaller. When I realized that the streets were narrowing, I also realized we were within feet of our destination. I pressed on—that is, until my wife gently pointed out that ahead of us were a set of steps. I had run out of road and out of space to turn around. The GPS got us to our destination—I just wasn't sure I could ever leave!

Eventually, with the help of two of the kindest Croatians I met on that trip, I was able to free our car from the trap of my own rule-following folly. I was fortunate that we fared better than others in similar GPS mishaps. At least I didn't have to get my car towed from the stairs by police and parking officials, as one driver did in New York (West Sider, 2013). *That* would have been embarrassing!

We tend to follow authoritative directions without question. Most of the time, our rule-following nature serves us well. Other times, though, such rule following disorients us from our ultimate goal. As one woman admitted after she followed GPS directions on a day-long trip through another part of Europe (for a journey that should have taken her a couple of hours and ended with the police searching for her as a missing person), "I admit it's a little weird, but I was distracted" (Hansen, 2013). Rather than recognizing our surroundings, thinking critically about the world around us and our relative location within it, we trust the directions—sometimes to our peril.

Maps versus Directions

Why do you need this book? You already have the handbook that corresponds to your particular edTPA assessment. Within the handbook, you have access to resources helping you to organize your thinking. There are specific suggestions telling you what to do and what to write as well as rubrics showing you how your work will be scored. You need this book, however, because the edTPA handbook you are using is similar to a set of directions; it is intended to take you from Point A to Point B. This book instead represents your map. Maps and sets of directions each have their own advantages and disadvantages; they each have their own way of approaching the same destination and can be used to complement each other.

Declarative directions can be comforting, especially in high-stakes situations. Though people usually do not like to be told what to do, being told what to do in unfamiliar situations can be reassuring. Many teacher candidates may be similarly comforted to have a set of directions, in the form of the edTPA handbook, explicitly telling them how to approach the edTPA portfolio. As teacher candidates across the United States are being required to pass teacher performance assessments to determine their eligibility for certification, this hurdle represents a high-stakes situation. They have already invested four or more years in college and/or graduate school, time and money in state-mandated test requirements, and hours in practice teaching experiences. The natural tendency for these candidates is to follow the directions found within the handbook.

Maps, on the other hand, offer a different perspective. Unlike linear, step-by-step directions, maps allow you to see the bigger picture. A map still shows you where Point A and Point B are, but it shows you everything in between as well. You have a bit more autonomy in choosing an appropriate route and can evaluate which path is the best for you to take personally. This book will show you the bigger picture. You will be able to feel more confident in making choices in your classroom by seeing the different ways that you can approach and reach your final destination—a successful edTPA score.

Your edTPA Map: The Structure of This Book

This book (your map) will review educational theories, pedagogical strategies, and best practices that are most applicable to the edTPA. None of the theories and strategies discussed here will be in as great a depth as you had first learned them in your coursework. Instead, we are showing you the way these ideas all connect and the way they collectively work to support your teaching and portfolio preparation. We will provide you with opportunities for self-reflection and practice to better prepare yourself for your edTPA submission. Continuing with our map analogy, be sure to watch for these text features to make the most of your use of this book:

- *Orientation: You Are Here.* Anyone who has had to use a map at a theme park or local mall will know that finding the "You Are Here" place marker is the best place to begin. This specific part of each chapter will provide you with a brief statement as to what you should already know before proceeding and what you will gain by reading the chapter.
- *Landmarks.* When navigating, we use landmarks because they stand out and are familiar to us. Throughout each chapter, we will identify specific aspects of your teacher preparation program (that should be familiar to you) and relate them to the completion of the edTPA. We have seen many student teachers fail to make the connection that the edTPA is merely assessing the best teaching practices they already have in place. These landmarks are designed to draw your attention to the connections that exist between what you already do in the classroom and what is required of you in the edTPA.
- *Planning Pathways.* Within each chapter, we will challenge you to begin planning your own path toward edTPA completion. Specific activities have been designed, based on our experiences with edTPA, to encourage you to problem-solve and overcome some design challenges other students have faced.

- *Scale.* On maps, scale is used to indicate the relationship between sizes or distances on the map to the actual sizes or distances on Earth's surface. Wherever you see the **SCALE** mark in the text, it will highlight for you a specific relationship between the text and your edTPA portfolio.
- *Orientation: Where Are You Now?* As each chapter begins with a "You Are Here" marker, each chapter ends with the reflective question, "Where Are You Now?" Use the reflective questions and activities in this section to determine how your understanding and approach to teaching and the edTPA have changed.

While your edTPA submission is yours and yours alone, this book is intended to enhance your decision-making ability in terms of planning, instruction, and assessment. No one strategy is universally applicable; every teaching context, teacher candidate, and classroom of students is different. This map will guide you to better understand the edTPA so that you can make the best choices for yourself and for your students.

CHAPTER 1

Beyond Compliance

ORIENTATION
You Are Here

At this point, you may have just finished your coursework and are ready to begin student-teaching, or maybe you are just beginning the first foundational courses for your education major. In either case, you are most likely thinking about how the edTPA will tie in to your teacher preparation coursework and are probably nervous about how the results of this assessment will impact your ability to begin your career. As soon as you begin student-teaching, you should also immediately begin thinking about your edTPA portfolio. Get to know what is expected of you because, before long, you will be completing and submitting your portfolio.

This chapter will give you insight into why we have teacher performance assessments like the edTPA, how they have evolved over time, and what you can do to empower yourself as you complete the assessment.

Taking the Fear out of edTPA

Most people encounter teacher performance assessments toward the end of their teacher preparation programs. These assessments serve as the last hurdle for students in most states to earn their teaching certification. In this sense, teacher performance assessments are very high-stakes tests.

Unfortunately, "high-stakes test" is the beginning and end of most people's contextual understanding of teacher performance assessments. Recently, when we asked a group of pre-service teachers why they had to complete and pass the edTPA (a national teacher performance assessment), their responses mirrored this understanding:

"To get my teaching certificate."

"To prove I am a qualified teacher."

"To prove I know what I'm doing in the classroom."

Their ideas and the language they used were not inaccurate, but they were certainly incomplete. Most importantly, they illustrated an unfortunate phenomenon of high-stakes tests—people exaggerate what the tests can say about test-takers' ability.

The edTPA, in this instance, can't prove anything about you as a teacher. Over the course of the assessment tasks, you are only providing a scorer with a sequence of a few lesson plans, one to two short videos of your instruction, and some student work samples. The edTPA actually calls the unit a "learning segment," and it is right to do so. You are submitting just a snapshot of your instruction, a segment of your instruction and your students' learning. It proves nothing about your dedication to your students, your future success as a teacher, or your deep commitment to the profession (Pecheone & Whittaker, 2016). Don't let the edTPA have that much power. It is an assessment—nothing more.

That doesn't mean that it is not an important assessment; surely, most teacher candidates' teaching certifications ride on passing such state-required teacher performance assessments. The weight of these assessments is not in what they "prove" about you but in what they demand of our profession in relation to our system of education. While there is certainly an element of compliance for you as a teacher candidate, understanding the history of these assessments not only helps us to understand their importance in clearer ways but also helps us to complete (and pass) them with greater fidelity to their purposes.

From Facts to Pedagogical Content Knowledge

A favorite sentence starter for teacher candidates trying to explain the importance of teacher performance assessments is, "Especially in the world today . . ." (or some variation of the sort). Teacher candidates often finish this sentence with claims like, "we need to have a better prepared teacher workforce," "we need to show we can actually teach," and "we need to know our stuff." There are two interesting points to be gleaned from these responses. First, the common sentence starter suggests that good teachers were not as needed in the past. Somehow, previous generations did not have the need for as highly qualified and skilled teachers as we have today.

This exceptionalism of the present is obviously false. Political, social, economic, and moral issues have consistently plagued human societies. In most cases, better education for greater numbers of students was a solution (though we can also argue that power structures have been and continue to be excruciatingly slow in their acceptance of a more inclusive student body). Such an education to an increasingly diverse set of students necessitated the best trained teachers of every generation. While our current local, national, and global issues may be unique, the only "exceptionality argument" is for *different* education, as *better* education is something that has been consistently sought (Ravitch, 2014).

We should be careful with how unique we find our current situation, though, a second interesting note from the preceding comments. While it is easy to argue that previous generations have never contended with the internet, smartphones, social media, and the enormity of choice we have in everyday decisions, the struggles our society faces are simply more amplified than before (Newport, 2016). For example, John Dewey (1916, 1938) developed his philosophy of education in the context of rapid industrialization (which brought new technologies like the automobile), rapid immigration, world war, and economic upheaval—a context that is familiar to many people around the world today. To argue that education did not demand the best of teachers in that context belies the reality that we face similar challenges.

A more inclusive view in contrast to saying we need "better teachers" would be to suggest that we need to better assess the skills that teachers possess because our tools and understandings of instruction and learning are more sophisticated. We can better explain teachers' strengths and weaknesses because we have more information about, and skill to assess, teaching and learning than we did even five years ago.

A Brief History of Teacher Performance Assessments

Modern teacher candidate assessments in the United States can be traced back to the 1800s, when states first implemented tests of teacher candidates' content knowledge (Shulman, 1986). Vestiges of these tests are seen in the various content tests that candidates are required to pass (e.g., the Praxis

Core and state-created multisubject content tests). Like today, the tests of the 1800s assessed knowledge of various math, English/grammar, science, and social studies facts. These assessments mirrored the Core classes that pre-service teachers were responsible to take and teach, providing a cultural content knowledge for teachers.

As we have learned more about how students learn and process information, such tests have evolved. Today, most content tests include sections that require candidates to evaluate student work samples, identifying and creating plans to remediate student misconceptions. Incorporating such tasks with content knowledge has brought these tests closer to approximating the knowledge and skills that teachers must have to even appropriately transmit knowledge, what Lee Shulman (1986) refers to as *pedagogical content knowledge*. We know (as did teachers two centuries ago, although they probably couldn't explain the cognitive mechanisms) that information is not seamlessly transferred between teachers and students—it isn't a process of information downloading (or the banking model, as Paulo Freire [1970] describes it). Rather, as information is taken up by students and integrated into their own experiences, perceptions, and understandings, misconceptions arise and understandings are distorted (Kintsch, 1998). Teaching requires more than content knowledge alone and more than "teaching skills" alone (Rodriguez & Fitzpatrick, 2014); teachers must have command of the most useful models of instructional explanations (Leinhardt, 2010) and the capacities to bring forward "alternative forms of representation, some of which derive from research whereas others originate in the wisdom of practice" (Shulman, 1986, p. 9), when students struggle. Including such tasks on teacher performance exams confirms teachers' abilities to identify such misconceptions and appropriately plan to address them.

But even these tests are not really enough. Being able to identify a misconception in such a particular context relies heavily on content knowledge but not necessarily on a teacher's ability to actually teach students to reconsider their conceptions. Such tests continue to be modeled on a "banking system" of education (Freire, 1970). The assumption is that if a teacher can identify a misconception and reexplain it, then students should be able to understand the new explanation and be successful on some measure of learning.

We know from experience and from research that this isn't true, even for highly capable students. As Ken Bain (2004) explains, difficult concepts can be expertly taught by professors who have dedicated their lives to a particular topic and still find that a majority of students return to their former misconceptions. Even after the professor identifies and remediates the misconception, students still struggle to change their beliefs about the universe. Concepts, it turns out, are stubborn and do not want to change.

So, to the extent that it is important for teachers to know a depth and breadth of content knowledge *and* to know how to identify at least common misconceptions related to that content knowledge, such an assessment regimen still falls short of saying anything about a teacher's ability to teach. Such tests may produce statistically valid and reliable results, but they are missing the most critical element of education, an element that makes teaching a wonderfully messy and fulfilling endeavor—the students.

Direct Measures of Teaching

While teacher tests began as early as the 1850s, student teaching was not standard practice in most states until the late 1930s. Even then, it took until the 1960s and '70s for almost all states to require a clinical practice component to their programs, and even then, standards varied widely (Schneider, 2011). Thus, it hasn't been until recently that schools of education, state officials, or school administrators had any direct measures of teaching performance prior to certification and hire. This lack of teaching evidence continued to reinforce the idea that the information in a teacher's brain was the most important asset in the classroom.

As student teachers began practicing their instructional acumen during clinical practice, however, universities began to assess their student teachers in the classroom. Often, supervisors would use a homegrown rubric to assess student teachers' general knowledge, classroom management, and classroom climate. Post-observation conferences often related to what the teacher could do better next time, particularly focusing on establishing effective routines and procedures. Learning to teach was mainly an apprenticeship of observation (Lortie, 1975).

What was absent from these conversations was any genuine information about what the students learned. Even though teachers have assigned and collected homework and classwork for generations, teaching supervisors rarely looked at it or helped the student teachers to analyze it as data to drive instruction. The assumption was that the teacher candidate would assess the correctness of the answers and assign grades accordingly—"grading" was simple, and there was nothing to discuss. This mindset continues to be prevalent in classrooms today (Bower & Thomas, 2013).

Teachers, supervisors, and the public continued to reify a culture of assessment of learning. Tests, essays, quizzes, and reports were meant to assess students' learning of material taught in class. Failure to score well solely reflected a student's lack of mastery of content or skills; little more could be said of the work (Labaree, 2010; Ravitch, 2014, 2016). Yet teachers have long sat on a treasure-trove of data related to public policy initiatives, instrumental interventions, and teaching methods—formative assessment data in the form of student comments, worksheets, exit slips, and the like. With those data, teachers could assess students' progress to support, scaffold, and develop student learning. Paul Black and Dylan Wiliam (1998) refer to this as *assessment for learning*.

The use of formative assessment data to inform teachers' reflection of their own instruction, the extent to which students did learn the material, and the extent to which they needed further support philosophically aligned with what teachers generally believed. First, formative classroom assessments provide more useful and meaningful data than high-stakes tests. Second, understanding students' learning in microsettings allows for an insight into students' thought processes—the driver of concepts and mindsets. And third, learning is not a steadily progressing pursuit. There are "Aha" moments and long sections of comparative cognitive drought. Understanding when each happen, and the mechanisms for the Aha moments, can be found in formative assessment work samples.

And here is where teacher performance assessments have added a new, important layer to preparing teachers. Beginning in the 1980s, schools of education began implementing the teacher work sample methodology, which asked teacher candidates to plan and teach a two to five-week unit of instruction, assessing student learning and revising those plans throughout the duration. This length of time enabled teacher candidates to engage in the practice and challenge of teaching at the level of "the unit," far beyond the lesson-planning assignments typically assigned in teacher preparation coursework (Schalock & Schalock, 2011). Beyond the obvious importance of content knowledge and beyond the critical skills and dispositions needed to develop and sustain a productive, positive classroom culture, teacher performance assessments assess those components' impact on student growth and learning in *real time* (Darling-Hammond, 2017). Relying on formative assessments, teacher performance assessments require teacher candidates to demonstrate their knowledge of real students and their content expertise to assess what they can do as teachers to actually support and develop student learning; in essence, they allow teacher candidates to assess their own decision-making capacities (Kohler, Henning, & Usma-Wilches, 2008). Most importantly, though, they allow teachers to demonstrate some of the good work they are doing for students every day.

The edTPA

The edTPA is a specific performance assessment that asks candidates to plan, implement, and assess their instruction. The edTPAs for secondary education candidates have three parts,* called *Tasks*, aligning with those three purposes. You will pick one class to focus on as you complete your edTPA portfolio. In Task 1, candidates are asked to (1) discuss the classroom and the students you have selected to complete the edTPA with, (2) provide a three- to five-lesson learning segment for that class along with associated materials, and (3) craft a commentary in which you reflect on your instructional planning decisions.

Task 2 requires candidates to provide video of their instruction. Candidates are generally able to post one or two videos

---

* If you have friends who are completing the Elementary Education edTPA, they will tell you there are four tasks. For them, that is correct. The edTPA has handbooks for elementary education candidates that assess their abilities to teach both math and ELA. This is not what you are asked to do as secondary education candidates.

of instruction that are no less than three minutes long and no more than twenty minutes long in total. For example, you might provide a nine-minute example of direct instruction and a ten-minute example of students working in cooperative groups, totaling nineteen minutes of total instruction. Your instruction will showcase your ability to use academic language with students, your pedagogy during the lesson, and the classroom environment you have helped to create. Again, you will complete a commentary in which you will reflect on your instruction.

In Task 3, you will present student work samples for three of your students and illustrate the aggregate formative assessment data from your class. The edTPA refers to this assessment as summative because it is meant to reflect the sum of the learning in that three- to five-lesson learning segment. While they are technically correct in calling this a summative assessment, it is more closely aligned to a formative assessment than an end-of-unit exam, as we will discuss in chapter 3. You will also complete a reflective commentary for Task 3.

In total, the edTPA asks candidates to demonstrate a learning cycle. These learning cycles are distinct across disciplines, but the broad strokes of the assessment are the same. The edTPA is looking for you to demonstrate your ability to plan, teach, and assess your students in a thoughtful manner—that's it!

Reducing Fear

So, with the positives that performance assessments bring to the more authentic professionalization of teaching, why is there so much fear around them—particularly around the edTPA? Again, the high-stakes nature of these assessments is to blame. "It positions teachers as valuable and capable professionals, but embraces elements of compliance-based accountability. . . . It emphasizes performance and practice, but exists as a high-stakes, summative assessment" (Cochran-Smith et al., 2018, p. 132). The direct link between doing well on performance assessments and certification is an extrinsically motivating factor for completing the assessment well. This link makes performance assessments summative rather than formative. Thus, there is little room for a growth mindset to be applied (Dweck, 1999, 2006). Growth, development, and learning are not the purposes of the assessment, as seen through the eyes of the big "stick" of the "noncertification through failure" paradigm.

Focus on the Extrinsic Motivation

If you are fearful of the edTPA, you are not alone and have every right to those feelings. Not only do your teacher candidate colleagues feel the same fears, but scholarship continues to emerge citing such fears and their negative impacts on teacher candidates and teaching performance (DeMoss, 2017). Like stress, a little fear isn't bad—it keeps you on your toes and forces you to do some of your best work. But, also like stress, too much fear is detrimental to performance and morale. Human beings deserve to thrive through challenge and acceptance (Palmer, 2007). To the extent that teacher performance assessments create detrimental fear, and their results are used as single-factor indicators of "good teaching," they create an immoral and anti-research-based hurdle that harms the profession.

Fortunately, we don't need to view high-stakes performance assessments only through the paradigm of external motivators (e.g., certification). To the extent that you, your professors, school personnel, and policy makers can create more humane and research-based uses of performance assessments, the better. But on an individual level, you also have the ability right now to view performance assessments through intrinsically motivating factors, factors that are embedded into the work of teaching already.

Focus on the Intrinsic Motivation

Richard Ryan and Edward Deci's (2000) work on motivation has concluded that there are three aspects to any task or event that enable intrinsic motivation to flourish: autonomy, mastery, and purpose (see fig. 1.1).

When we focus on developing our intrinsic motivation toward task completion, we are more fulfilled in our work and are more productive. This productivity comes from the increased practice that individuals engage in when they are intrinsically motivated to do something. In other words, people who are intrinsically motivated to do something are willing to put in more independent practice (work) on a task than people who are only extrinsically motivated to complete the task. That extra time spent working, playing with, and engaging the

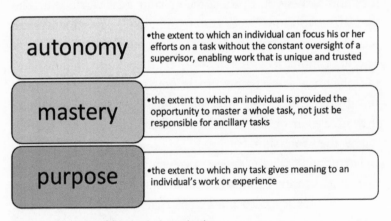

Figure 1.1. Factors enabling intrinsic motivation

task creates a better product than any time spent completing a task to overcome an externally imposed hurdle. While performance assessments are certainly externally imposed hurdles, the good news is that we can shift our paradigm to focus on intrinsic motivations by focusing on areas where we can display autonomy, mastery, and purpose in the work.

Areas of autonomy. Unlike traditional standardized tests, performance assessments require individuals to demonstrate actual examples of practice. As such, they cannot be overly specific about the exact types of knowledge or contexts where the real-world practice is performed. That means that the candidate, not the scorer, has control over the context of the performance. This is no small bit of autonomy; having control over the context of learning gives you the ability to select the classroom, the class, the instructional materials, and the curricular concepts related to planning, instruction, and assessment. These are critical aspects of the teaching process that you have near-complete control over.

As we have worked with candidates, though, there are some contextual caveats that make this autonomous space different between one classroom placement and another. For example, some pre-service teachers have cooperating teachers that clearly define what should be taught and how it should be taught in their classroom. Others find that they are placed in a particular class where they feel less comfortable with the content than they would with other topics. And still other pre-service teachers find that they are in the process of "learning up" to teaching a particular population of students as they are also trying to plan and teach a performance assessment unit.

In these cases, teacher candidates still have some power, if not as much as they would like. Through the network of university clinical supervisors, cooperating teachers, and instructional support staff, teacher candidates have the ability to discuss lesson innovations with other educators to meet performance assessment requirements, find an alternate placement in a content area more aligned with the teacher candidate's expertise, and co-plan with support staff to meet students' needs while also fulfilling the assessment requirements. Remember, autonomy doesn't mean you can do whatever you want; it means that you have control. The supports that your teacher preparation program has set up to ensure your future success are available to you to make the process as autonomous as possible.

PLANNING PATHWAYS

Recognizing the autonomy you retain in this process will probably result in greater self-confidence and a more effective portfolio. Generate a list of the factors you can control during the learning segment for which you will write your assessment portfolio.

Areas of mastery. While you are not a master teacher, you have certainly been developing mastery over your instructional practice in order to get to the clinical practice portion of your program. In-program progressions have guided you through a specific thinking process about the iterative nature of planning, teaching, and assessing. All of the feedback that you have received from your program faculty, cooperating teachers, and students have honed your mastery of this thing we call *teaching.*

Most accredited programs require students to complete at least one lesson-planning assessment, one unit-planning assessment, and smaller portfolio assignments and micro-teaching activities throughout their time in-program. These assignments, together with the experiential work that many students complete throughout their programs, prepare teacher candidates for the types of roles and responsibilities that practicing teachers have. *They are also the types of activities that are assessed during performance assessments.* Though rubric standards, lesson-plan outlines, and assessment criteria may vary, the general format of such in-program learning mirrors what is expected of in-service teachers and what is expected of teacher candidates' performance on in-program assessments.

This relationship between education courses and field hours is critical to both improved teaching performance and improved performance on teacher performance assessments. The field is recognizing that the more time that teacher candidates spend in quality clinical practice experiences, the better prepared they are for teaching (Borden, Preskill, & DeMoss, 2012; Polakow-Suransky, Thomases, & DeMoss, 2016). More time in schools means more time to learn the intricacies of planning for the students and the content simultaneously, more time to think deeply about the curriculum and what should be assessed, more time to learn to collaborate with school support staff, and more time to experience interacting with students as a teacher. The time teacher candidates spend in schools is coordinated through schools of education, where there is a shared understanding of the learning outcomes. This symbiotic relationship between education courses and field placements is often an underappreciated aspect of teacher preparation. What you have learned across these experiences has been a process of mastery that you will continue through any performance assessment and long into your teaching career.

Areas of purpose. While performance assessments certainly do not give your life meaning and purpose (or at least we hope they don't!), they *are* tasks related to the purpose of our profession. As we argued earlier, no performance assessment can capture the entirety of our work as teachers. They cannot capture all of the thoughtful planning, inspired instruction, and meaningful assessment that goes on in the class; these assessments can only see part of the final product. Even more importantly, though, performance assessments often don't even look at some of the most important individual effects a teacher can have on a student's life. To our knowledge, no performance assessment captures the "lunch-period pep talk," the after-school homework session, or the Friday-night show of support at the school's sporting event, where you informally stay with your students and share some school spirit. Again, performance assessments might pick up some of the outcomes of such work (e.g., higher student engagement, increased academic performance, and improved student-teacher rapport), but they don't capture these other equally meaningful moments.

All hope is not lost! Just because an assessment does not capture those aspects of our profession that we deeply value doesn't mean that we can find no value in fully engaging the assessment. Each performance assessment task relates to a critical aspect of teaching that can and should be influenced by our consistent, focused purpose as teachers to help students develop their capacities to be thoughtful, engaged, and ethical members of society.

Whether it be the edTPA, a professional/tenure portfolio, or an application for national board certification, our field has defined four general areas where our overall passion for teaching can be delineated. Three of these take place directly in the classroom and are cyclical in nature; a change in one will have a cascade effect on the others. Planning engaging material for

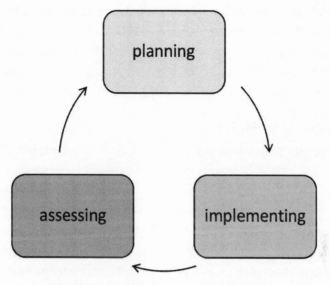

Figure 1.2. The iterative segments of the teaching process

the students in our classes, implementing aligned instruction in a positive classroom environment, and assessing students *for* learning are three parts of the whole process that is teaching (see fig. 1.2). The fourth area, engaging in professional communities, has a profound impact on the previous three. Planning effective lessons will promote better instruction. When the instruction is then assessed authentically, teachers can use the data to further drive instruction. Our ultimate purpose of guiding and developing students' capacities derives from these four professional activities. In these activities, then, we find some of our passion for teaching. While not all of us are passionate about each of these in the same way, we can all find our passions within these activities and their subsets.

Performance assessments are opportunities to share an aspect of your purpose through the passion you bring to these activities. We can tap into that purpose while engaging the assessment by focusing our resources not on the assessment but on our students, demonstrating the great work that we do to scaffold and support their capacity building. If we do that, the performance assessment is little more than just another day's work—with a bit more writing and angst.

Beyond Compliance

Performance assessments are our field's best attempts to better understand how you as a teacher think, teach, and collaborate. Many times, these are high-stakes tests that require some form of compliance. When we only think about these assessments as tests of compliance (e.g., trying to give "them" what they want to see so that we can move on with our lives), that extrinsic motivation creates more fear, stress, and uninspired instruction. We must recognize that teacher performance assessments aren't easy, single-answer tests; they ask us to engage in the complex problem solving that is teaching. "Solving complex problems is a messy business—and mindlessly ticking boxes is a sure sign of falling into the quick fix" (Honore, 2013, p. 241).

We move beyond compliance by recognizing that we are *full, whole* teachers before, during, and after the assessment. The work that we do every day is more meaningful than a score. That meaning derives from our abilities to customize our working environment with our students. To this end, you have more latitude when completing a performance assessment of your teaching. Even beyond your own capacities to define the environment in which you teach (from the classroom environment that you create with your students to the instructional decisions you make about how students engage in the material), the rubrics lend themselves to focus on creative teaching through constructivist, culturally relevant instruction. Mistilina Sato (2014) argues that these design components create space for both culturally relevant and disciplinary-specific pedagogies. "Ultimately, these patterns convey an image of quality teaching through the edTPA rubrics that is highly individualized, using research, theory, and data to justify learning approaches that emphasize student agency and promote disciplinary-specific thinking" (Clayton, 2017, p. 90). Rather than encouraging candidates to adhere to a checkbox model as the edTPA handbook directions portray, the rubrics (the ways that your work will be assessed) are open to expressions of autonomy, mastery, and purpose.

SCENIC DETOUR
Fostering Creativity

In customizing our instructional spaces, and recognizing that that customization is an option, we are able to think more clearly, calmly, and aspirationally about our work as teachers. There is an interesting study that Dr. Michael Housman explains that demonstrates this point (Pinsker, 2015). He noticed that the people who were the most creative, explored the most possibilities, and engaged the most interesting ideas all used Chrome as their internet browser. This was a really interesting observation because one wouldn't suspect that the type of browser you use would make someone more or less creative. And, in fact, it doesn't; the browser itself is just a tool.

The reason that the browser mattered was because Chrome wasn't the preset browser for any of the subjects' computers. The people who were using Chrome had to think beyond the preset application on their computers to customize their digital experiences. Instead of using the browser just to achieve an end (searching the internet, checking an email, etc.), the people who put the effort into customizing their experiences created a space that fostered creativity.

Surely some of the people who used Safari or Explorer actually preferred those browsers to Chrome, but that is not the whole of the story. The lesson is that when we are directly focused on achievement (getting tasks done as efficiently as possible), we neglect to create customizable spaces— spaces that foster creativity. "When achievement motivation goes sky-high, it can crowd out originality: The more you value achievement, the more you come to dread failure. Instead of aiming for unique accomplishments, the intense desire to succeed leads us to strive for guaranteed success" (Grant, 2016, pp. 10–11).

A compliance view of performance assessments harms us and our students. Both deserve better.

Summary

It is understandable that you may have a great amount of anxiety about passing the edTPA, as your licensure and potential career are directly related to the results. This chapter, however, has aimed to support you through the process by helping you realize that assessing teacher candidates has a long history of development that works to continually improve the quality of teachers who make it into classrooms. Though the process may seem daunting, it does serve a purpose: it shows what a great teacher you are becoming! You have the ability to affect the results of your submission by carefully and purposefully controlling the learning environment you provide for your students. The remaining chapters of this book will help you determine how to best represent yourself through your assessment portfolio.

ORIENTATION

Where Are You Now?

1   What are some of the thoughts and feelings you experienced when you first learned you would have to pass the edTPA to earn your license for teaching? Have these views changed as a result of reading this chapter, considering the assessment through a new perspective?

2   Compare your extrinsic motivation for passing the edTPA to your intrinsic motivation for passing the assessment. What factors motivate you? How can you harness your intrinsic motivation to more fully and successfully engage the assessment?

CHAPTER 2

Planning for Instruction

ORIENTATION

You Are Here

By reading chapter 1, you have gained an understanding of the purpose of teacher performance assessments. Additionally, you may have changed the lens through which you view these assessments, which will help you in successfully approaching the construction of your portfolio.

This chapter will help you begin to plan for your portfolio by reviewing concepts of strategic unit planning. The important roles of national and state standards, authentic assessment, and objective alignment will be discussed.

Purpose of Education

Why do you want to be a teacher? Regardless of your specific answer, your response probably includes a desire to make a positive difference in the lives of children. You have probably been inspired (either through a positive or a negative experience) by a particular teacher in your own education, leading you to want to be able to make a positive impact yourself. The connection you can make with your students is the driving force that leads people to the teaching profession.

Yet there is another equally important question that you need to ask, especially as you complete your teacher preparation program and begin thinking about life in the classroom: Why do you teach students? This question recenters the focus from you to your students. This question requires some thought as to what you expect the outcome of all of your hard work to be. What should you and your students expect to get out of all of this?

LANDMARK

Early in your teacher preparation program, you probably wrote a personal philosophy of education. If you have it, look back at what you wrote. What drives your ideas about teaching and learning?

Take some time to read "new to you" philosophies of education. You might find Parker Palmer's (2007) *Courage to Teach* or Nel Noddings's (2013) *Education and Democracy in the 21st Century* to be enlightening.

As you progress through your student teaching experience, continue to think about your philosophy of education. Update this document from time to time as you synthesize scholarly research and your own teaching experiences. You may find it useful to review before going on job interviews as you will probably be asked about it by potential employers.

Students ask this question in a different way: Why do I have to learn? or Why do I have to go to school? The responses they receive from the adults around them will probably be quick replies that don't really address the importance of the question. Children have to attend school because it is a cultural norm, a societal expectation, and it is enforced by law. Parents may elaborate that they want their children to learn or to make their families proud. Even parents' answers can vary. While most think that the main goal of education if to prepare students academically (45 percent), many also think it is to prepare students for work (25 percent) or to prepare them to be good citizens (26 percent); 4 percent of parents don't know! (Walker, 2016). These responses are less than satisfying. Much as we discussed in chapter 1, engaging in activities simply to fulfill an obligation is rather unmotivating. For those students who hear and believe these answers, we should recognize the courage and willpower that it takes for them to make it to school each morning.

Among the many more satisfying answers, an important aspect is what learning can contribute to our students' future, which we can see as a summarizing theme in the poll responses just mentioned. We teach children, representatives of a future generation, the knowledge, skills, and dispositions they will need to be successful independently of adults (both individually and collectively) in the future (Dewey, 1916). School is not simply a place to send children while their parents are working. It is not a place where children spend ten months of the year because that is what has traditionally been done. Schooling and learning have a greater purpose—many purposes, actually. Among the most important is to teach students how to think and communicate in critical and reflective ways.

As Tony Wagner (2008) argues, mastery of basic skills is simply not enough for individuals to succeed in the twenty-first century; technology and human innovation are such that nearly all jobs and societal obligations require individuals who can manage complexity: "Thus, work, learning, and citizenship in the twenty-first century demand that we all know how to *think*—to reason, analyze, weigh evidence, problem-solve—and to *communicate effectively*" (p. xxiii). The next time you are questioned about what you do in the classroom, be sure to explain that you have instructed future engineers, scientists, nurses, CEOs, and government officials. Perhaps you will have also inspired a future teacher to follow in your footsteps.

Beginning with Reading, Writing, and Thinking in Mind

Fortunately, centuries of scholastic efforts have provided us with the academic disciplines. These disciplines provide specific ways for us to read, write, and think about observable and unobservable phenomena. Too often, academic disciplines get a bad rap. When a set of ideas is dismissed as "too academic" or as *just* an academic argument, it is often from a misunderstanding of what the disciplines offer individuals and society. The academic disciplines formed as groups of like-minded thinkers began to explore various physical and metaphysical phenomena in consistent, reasoned ways (Krishnan, 2009). They formed methodologies through which we can reliably explore our environments and make predictions about the future.

Out of these ways of thinking have come ways of reading and writing that serve as the basis for effective communication across a range of fields. For example, the ways that scientists and social scientists identify and define variables enables them to isolate causal agents within a system (Christie & Maton, 2011). The ways that historians and journalists contextualize and corroborate evidence drive both their writing style and the ways in which they approach written text (Wineburg, 2018). Appropriately learning these ways of thinking, reading, and writing and then later appropriately mixing and matching these techniques allow our society to create and innovate. We may not know what society will look like ten years from now, but we can shape students' ways of thinking about the world by explicitly sharing disciplinary ways of knowing (epistemologies) with them. These epistemologies aren't merely for academics—they are the basis for authentic learning and innovation.

Levels of Planning

These disciplinary ways of knowing are consistently revised and updated in the forms of new methodological research and new curricular standards (Parkay, 2016). Through professional associations, disciplinary scholars, teacher educators, teachers, and administrators coconstruct frameworks based on feedback and insight from leading professionals that guide what students should know and be able to do within the disciplines. In the United States, these frameworks include curricular standards that are then adopted, revised, and contextualized by state school boards.

Each state has a set of standards that students must learn and be able to apply before the end of each school year. To help students meet these standards, the individual school districts approve a curriculum for each subject at each grade level that will include a scope and sequence. The scope gives teachers an idea of both how deeply and how broadly into each topic they need to delve with their students. The sequence provides a basic timeline for instruction so that teachers in the same grade level can stay together as they progress through the school year. The curriculum may also include resources and activity suggestions and is a good place to begin the planning phases of instruction (Parkay, 2016).

Once the teacher has determined what needs to be taught and when, they will begin planning a unit. The unit will encompass a broad topic that can be broken into shorter learning segments. These learning segments may take approximately three to five forty-five-minute lessons to complete. ***SCALE:*** ***It is the learning segment that you will need to prepare for your*** ***edTPA portfolio.***

For example, a math unit may be called "Expressions and Equations" and take students several school weeks to complete. Within this unit, there may be several learning segments related to solving one-step equations, evaluating expressions, using properties of operations, and analyzing models or graphs. Each learning segment will most likely be a series of three to five lessons that build toward the ultimate unit goal(s). An example from science could be seen in a unit about the Earth-moon-sun system that is broken into learning segments exploring seasons, day-night cycles, moon phases, eclipses, and tides. Each of these smaller learning segments takes a few days, or lessons, to complete and ultimately contributes to the students' understanding of the overall unit (the Earth-moon-sun system). Figure 2.1 shows the levels of planning from a national perspective down to an individual lesson within your classroom.

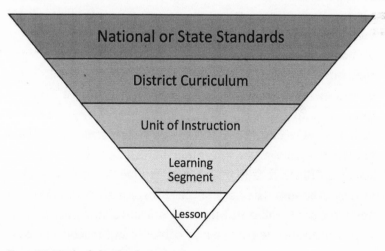

Figure 2.1. Levels of planning for instruction

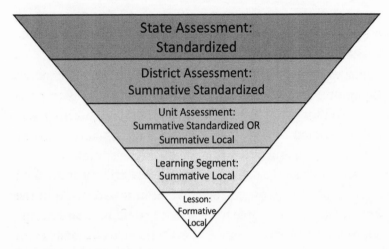

Figure 2.2. Levels of assessment

Levels of Assessing

Coinciding with the levels of planning, there are specific levels of assessment implicit in figure 2.1. These assessment levels are shown in figure 2.2. While various teacher preparation programs talk about these levels using slightly different terms, we can think about these levels of assessment in ways that mirror the purpose of the planning level.

Assessments are traditionally broken into two main categories, summative and formative, based on their purpose. *Summative assessments* are assessments *of* learning that occur at the end of an instructional planning level. They assess what students have cumulatively learned within that level. *Formative assessments*, on the other hand, are assessments *for* learning (Black & Wiliam, 1998) and may occur at any time during a lesson. They assess the progress that students are making toward the stated learning objective and are intended to provide valuable feedback to students and teachers so that teachers can continue to tailor instruction to best meet their students' needs.

The creation of assessments occurs at different levels as well. *Standardized assessments* are created and administered to produce information about how students' learning ranks against other students' learning, using psychometric methods (Wineburg, 2018). These assessments can be created by some large districts, state organizations, or educational testing companies. *Local assessments* are created by individual teachers for classroom use or by some school districts in the form of benchmark or other comparative exams. Local assessments may not be statistically valid or reliable, but they often provide information about student learning from work samples, making any findings from analysis more authentic to the students' context.

The assessments used in both the lesson plans and the learning segment of an edTPA portfolio are local; they are under your control as the teacher. Tied to the state-approved standards and your mastery objectives, these assessments provide you with authentic information about your students' progress toward those outcomes. You will learn more about how to plan both types of assessments in chapter 3.

Lesson Planning

Lesson plans are developed by teachers on the basis of (1) the intended outcome of the learning segment, (2) the content (knowledge, skills, and dispositions) required for students to reach the intended outcome, and (3) knowledge of the students as learners. A lesson that works for one class may not necessarily be the best option for a different class simply because the students within the classes may have different ability levels, prior experiences, and learning styles. Lesson-plan formats will also vary from teacher to teacher or from district to district depending on how strict the requirements are at the district level and what those requirements are. Some districts or evaluating administrators will require only a short synopsis of standards and lesson activities. Most will require these in addition to stated learning objectives, plans for differentiation, and plans for assessments. Lesson objectives may have different names in different teacher preparation programs or school districts, such as "learner outcomes" or "goals of instruction," but their meaning remains the same; objectives are the goals you expect your students to achieve by the end of the lesson.

LANDMARK

Ever notice that your professors use one lesson-plan format and your cooperating teacher uses another? And why do different schools and districts have varying formats?! It can be so frustrating!

Luckily, the edTPA does not require you to use any particular format. Your teacher preparation program probably has a format that it aligned to the edTPA for you. Use that if you can, even if you think that it is too much effort. The more you can demonstrate your instructional decisions via your lesson plans, the easier it is to see the coherence of your learning segment.

New teachers should expect to follow the very lengthy lesson-plan formats required by their teacher preparation programs. In doing so, you will be building a habit for standards alignment and differentiation. Eventually, you will be able to do these things without much extra thought or effort. As you internalize this process, you will be able to write shorter lesson plans over time.

If you are interested in the lesson plan we use with our students, please see appendix A.

Standards and Mastery Objectives

Standards delineate exactly what students need to *know* and *be able to do* at each grade level and within each subject area. They represent a way to ensure that the rigor and quality of instruction is equitable from classroom to classroom; if all teachers teach to the standards, all students have the same opportunity for learning.

How standards are developed. Standards are developed through partnerships among teachers, university faculty, industry leaders, and government officials. The process of writing new standards can take several years, allowing time for initial drafts to be communicated to all stakeholders. Feedback on the drafts will lead to multiple rounds of revisions before a final set of standards is released.

Individual states may adopt nationally released standards, such as the Next Generation Science Standards (NGSS) and the National Council for the Social Studies C3 Framework (Croddy & Levine, 2014), or they may use these sets of standards as frameworks on which they can build their own individual state standards (National Research Council, 2013). In either form of development, standards *do* take into account what industry leaders recommend that students need to know for their future careers as well as what current teachers know to be best practices. They are not merely written by a group of politicians, as so many educators falsely believe.

What do standards look like? Standards can follow different formats depending on the state and discipline for which they have

MS-LS2-3
• Develop a model to describe the cycling of matter and flow of energy among living and nonliving parts of an ecosystem.

Figure 2.3. Sample science standard based on Next Generation Science Standards framework (National Research Council, 2013)

been written; however, they will all have similar components to help you use them. Each standard should have a grade level for which it is intended, a code or number to differentiate it from others within the framework, and a description of a task that is expected of the student. It is important to note that the tasks called for in the standards are for the students to be able to do, not the teachers. Figure 2.3 shows an example of a science standard from the NGSS framework.

The central focus. Standards and the central focus of your learning segment work hand in hand. The standards tell you what you have to teach, but the central focus is your explanation for why you have to teach it. It allows you to focus your teaching around a central purpose. When looking over your standards, ask yourself why it is important for your students to know the corresponding knowledge and skills addressed in the standards in the context of your course. Will they be using this information as a foundation for even greater knowledge development later in the year? How does the information or skill prepare the students for future learning? Similarly, ask yourself why the knowledge and skills in the standard are important for students to know in relation to real-world application. Using a real-world connection will help you gain students' buy-in as they will understand the benefits they receive from your instruction as it relates to their lives. Make these connections explicit to your students as you deliver instruction. Across your lesson plan, utilize a "Central Focus" heading for yourself to organize your thoughts about the importance of the learning segment. In some ways, you can consider this section analogous to an introduction in a formal essay. It should introduce the topic you are about to cover and your main purpose in having to teach it.

The Power of Unit Planning

Stephen Covey (2004), one of this century's foremost business thinkers, argues that the first step toward effective action is to begin with the end in mind. This means that we need to create in our minds what we want to create in the world. Without this mental work, we will waste time and energy as we attempt to create in the physical world.

For a guide to the mental work of learning segment planning, see appendix B.

Many teachers fall into the bad habit of design justification; they find activities they think look interesting, cute, or fun and then try to find an objective and standard that match the activities. As little kids tinkering with small toys realize, the square peg won't fit into the round hole; nor does the "justified" standard fit into the lesson. This is poor practice and should be avoided. You will notice in figure 2.4 that choosing instructional strategies and activities is actually the last step in the planning process rather than the first step. Instruction is much more effective when planning takes place at the unit level with standards chosen first, what Grant Wiggins and Jay McTighe (2005) refer to as "backward design." You will be a more effective teacher if you start to ask yourself, "How can I help my students reach this standard?" instead of questioning,

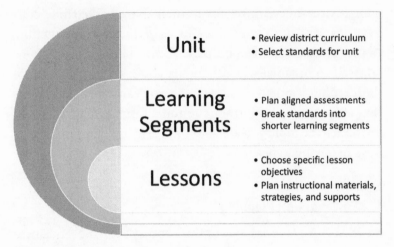

Figure 2.4. Process for creating standards-aligned units

"What standard could I use to match this activity?" The first question (associated with backward design) forces you to think about what your students need and how you can best support them, whereas the second question will only allow you to make a loose connection between instructional strategies and standards.

Using the standard to backward-design instruction. When you read over the sample standard in figure 2.3, you immediately think to yourself, "What will my students need to know or be able to do to accomplish this task?" The answers you come up with will probably be used as your daily objectives or learner outcomes. On the basis of this standard, we know that students must be able to do the following:

1 Describe what the living and nonliving parts of an ecosystem are

2 Describe the flow of energy through an ecosystem

3 Describe the cycling of matter within an ecosystem

4 Develop a model to show the movement of energy and matter among the ecosystem components

When you go back to the standard, it already tells you what your assessment will be ("Develop a model to describe . . ."). You must choose your daily activities so that your students will ultimately be able make a model demonstrating these connections and so that they will know how to describe them.

Now that you know your summative assessment, and you already broke down the standard into specific daily objectives, you can plan activities for each day to meet those objectives. Perhaps the first day would include a discussion and activity about living versus nonliving parts of an ecosystem. Have the students take a nature walk around the school and classify all of the things they find as living or nonliving. Have them work in groups to develop a list of traits that define living things. Pull the whole class back together to review these lists and come up with an accurate list for the whole class. For closure, review how living and nonliving things are different.

Day 2 requires the students to describe the flow of energy through an ecosystem. To warm up, discuss what energy is and where it comes from. You could have the students model a food web using balls of yarn and index cards showing what organism each student is pretending to be to demonstrate how energy is passed through the different trophic levels. Give them some situations that disrupt the food chain and discuss. For closure, have students review the objective by summarizing how energy is transferred in an ecosystem.

Day 3 could involve data gathering using an online simulation to have students examine the flow of matter in an ecosystem. They would collect data (for example, how much carbon dioxide is taken in or expelled by specific organisms) for different forms of matter. After students collect data, you have to review it with them looking for patterns (Did every group get the same results? Why?) and limitations (Why isn't a simulation as good as collecting field data?). They don't know how to analyze data this way without you leading them through it. Again, review your data as it pertains to your objective for the day.

Day 4 would be the assessment of your learning segment. Students might use construction paper to make posters demonstrating how energy and matter are transferred. This could also have been done using a 3-D diorama or online model. You will be looking to see that the model accurately shows living and nonliving components, energy originating at the sun and moving through the web, and one type of matter (oxygen, water, nutrients from soil) being cycled through the ecosystem.

Obviously this is a condensed, simplified version of the learning segment. It can *in no way* replace the careful planning you do with your specific students in your field placement, but it serves to demonstrate the thinking process you might go through as you design your learning segment to ensure you are meeting the standard.

PLANNING PATHWAYS

Create a sample learning segment by following the sequence discussed in the text. You can use the template in appendix B to help you. How is this process similar to or different from the process you have typically used in lesson planning?

Summary

As you prepare to pass the edTPA and ultimately begin your teaching career, your teaching effectiveness will be directly linked to your ability to plan and implement meaningful learning units—in this case, learning segments. These learning segments should be based on your district's curriculum, which will include a scope and sequence for including state standards into instruction. Your assessments will be developed, at the local level, to measure students' progress toward these standards and objectives. You have control over the learning segments you plan and implement, meaning that you have the ability to show your best work through your teacher performance assessment portfolio.

ORIENTATION

Where Are You Now?

1 Reflect on your own reason for entering the teaching profession. Why do you want to be a teacher? How will you use this to influence the way you teach your students?

2 How is a learning segment different from a unit? How are the two similar?

3 What role should standards play in the development of an instructional unit?

CHAPTER 3

Planning for Assessment

You Are Here

You have considered planning in relation to instruction, but as you began to see in chapter 2, planning cannot be isolated from assessment. These two paths represent an intersection on our map toward a successful edTPA score. We hope that you have started to consider and test different strategies for planning, instruction, and assessment. This intersection demands a focus on student thinking above pro forma participation—quality over quantity.

In this chapter, we will discuss how you can think about the role of assessment, particularly at the end of your learning segment. We will help you to determine the types of assessments that are appropriate to use in relation to your students, your content, and edTPA expectations.

Types of Assessments

You have already been introduced to multiple forms of assessment in chapter 2. You have also experienced many forms of assessment as a student yourself. As you begin your teaching career, it will be imperative that you understand these different forms and their associated purposes. We will discuss in chapter 7 how the data that you gather from these assessments can be used to monitor students' progress and mastery of content, measure students' use of academic language, plan interventions and supports, and develop plans for further instruction. These goals are the reason you assess your students. The type of assessment you plan and implement will be dependent on its purpose.

Formative Assessments: Measuring Students' Progress

While not weighed heavily in the edTPA, formative assessment (sometimes referred to as the "informal assessment") is arguably the most important type of assessment you will design. Formative assessments are those designed to measure students' *progress* toward learning goals as measured in summative assessments. This goal is implied by both names of the assessment type, as it is informative in nature and is used in informal, ungraded ways. As such, you will be designing these assessments yourself on the basis of your learning goals for your students. Generally, the better the formative assessments are created, the better the summative assessments are designed, which is critical for Tasks 1 and 3 of the edTPA.

Paul Black and Dylan Wiliam (2009) consider the use of formative assessment to be a staple of good pedagogy. While it may not be the only way in which teachers promote positive change in their classrooms, it certainly is an effective means because of the response and interaction quality you will experience. One of its strengths is the immediacy of the feedback you will receive from students; you will gain insight into their understanding, strengths, and weaknesses almost instantly. It also affords the teacher the ability to probe for further information or to adapt strategies as lessons progress. Finally, it is ongoing and offers a lot of data for the teacher to process.

The form of assessment you use for formative data will vary based on your goals, your particular teaching style, and the students within your classroom. Most likely, you will be using multiple forms within a given class period, such as engaging students in class discussions, reviewing students' graphic organizers, and evaluating students' exit slips to check for their progress toward specified goals. *SCALE: Rubric 5 is directly correlated with your use of assessment. Make sure that you explicitly state each form of assessment you plan to use throughout every lesson of your learning segment.* Your teaching will be most responsive to the learning taking place in your classroom when you use multiple assessments throughout each lesson to check for the progress being made by your students.

Formative assessment and cognitive apprenticeship. There is a tendency for teachers to assign "light assignments" (e.g., worksheets) and call them formative without a focus on process or progress. Such light assignments fail to address the spirit of formative assessment. Rather than opening a window into the students' thought processes, such assignments are either (1) skills-maintenance work, (2) organizational work, or (3) summative assessments in disguise.

There are times when you want to make sure that students maintain the skills that you have taught them. In these instances, you might provide them with a short assignment to keep them ready to use that skill in a future learning segment.

For example, a teacher might ask their students to complete a worksheet, asking them to solve equations and use the answers to appropriately color in a picture. While a light assignment, this example does not meet the definition of a formative assessment because there is no way (or desire to) assess the process by which students engaged in their work. The purpose of the assignment was to maintain students' procedural skills, not assess their progress.

There are also times when a teacher might use a graphic organizer to help their students organize their thoughts. There are certainly times when such organizers can be used as a formative assessment (e.g., when the students are just learning a new analysis skill and the organizer serves as the template). Many times, though, graphic organizers are simply there to help students organize their thoughts prior to doing the "real work." For example, if students already know how to read a short story and identify the plot, settings, characters, and so on, a graphic organizer might be helpful to organize this information. It would not serve as a formative assessment.

And still there are other times when assessments are "light" but there is no way to assess the product formatively. If a "Do Now" / warmup, exit ticket, or verbal check for understanding has only one right answer, that information fails to provide you with knowledge of students' progress or process. Rather than formative assessments, these are "light" summative assessments.

A quick test to determine whether an assessment is truly formative is to apply the *cognitive apprenticeship test*. Based on the cognitive apprenticeship literature (e.g., de Bruin, 2019; De La Paz et al., 2016), detailing how teachers can better model their thought processes for students, the *cognitive apprenticeship test* enables teachers to assess the degree to which a question can be explained.

The Cognitive Apprenticeship Test for Formative Assessments

1 Read the assessment question and pretend that it is on the board for you and the class to see.

2 Pretend that you are going to model how you (the expert) think through the problem of the question. If you can do this, proceed to the next step. *If you can't do this, the assessment is not a formative assessment.*

3 Thinking through the problem of the question, write your expert answer.

4 Using your expert answer as a guide, look back at your question. Is there a high probability that your students will be able to answer the question the way that you did? If so, you have a strong formative assessment. *If not, you might have a formative assessment, but you need to modify the prompt to elicit that answer.*

For example, if a class has been learning about the concept of democracy and its benefits, a high school teacher might ask, "Do democracies make the world safer?" The expert answer might explore the ways that democracies draw on the thoughts and wills of diverse populations, reducing the likelihood of widespread political oppression and increasing the likelihood of governments that think about diverse interests; as such, most people will not vote to go to war unjustly.* Reflecting on the original question, however, the teacher might realize that (a) the original question elicits yes/no answers and (b) the students were not prompted to think logically about the ways that democracies are formed and managed to answer this question. Thus, the teacher might reframe the question

---

* This is a Kantian argument, which the teacher might also include in their expert answer but might not expect students to be able to do.

to read, "How might the ways that democracies are governed make the world a safer place and possibly prevent war?"

PLANNING PATHWAYS

Look at one of your own lesson plans. Identify all of the formative assessments you may have planned for the class period. Are these activities truly formative assessments, or are they maintenance assignments? What other ways might you add in true formative assessments?

The reframed question allows the teacher to explore students' intellectual process and progress, identifying what they know about democracies and their impacts on world governance and peace. This reframed question meets the preceding criteria for formative assessment. If your assessment meets all of these criteria, then you have an assessment that allows you to really understand the progress and process that students are making toward understanding the content and/or using disciplinary ways of communicating.

What to do with your students' formative assessment work samples. The power of formative assessments lies in the immediacy of the feedback. The shorter the amount of time that students wait for direct feedback on their learning, the faster they can make adjustments to their thinking. But not all immediate feedback is equally useful. The usefulness of the feedback is tied directly to the objectives of the assessment.

In chapter 2, we argued that you need to "begin with the end in mind" by using your learning-segment standard to define the local summative assessment you will ask students to complete by the end of the learning segment. Once that

local summative assessment is defined, all of the other formative assessments will align to that one assessment. As such, the
feedback you provide students on any of the learning-segment
assessments will be in service to their proficiency on the local
summative assessment.

This alignment of feedback to assessments is more challenging in practice than it appears in theory. For example,
if the standard for your learning segment is Common Core
State Standard RH.9-10.6, "Compare the point of view of two
or more authors for how they treat the same topics, including
which details they include and emphasize in their respective
accounts," your local summative assessment will focus on some
type of comparison. Throughout your learning segment, your
formative assessments will focus on students' abilities to identify the perspectives of at least two authors and compare those
perspectives. In other words, your discussion questions, your
graphic organizers, and your exit slips will all serve to assess
your students' progress toward their comparison assignment.

Your feedback on your students' learning needs to be connected to their proficiency at comparing the perspectives of
the two authors. Important but incidental aspects of their
responses should be ignored (or at least not highlighted) in
service to their work on *comparing*. Aligning feedback with
assessment has at least three implications for the boundaries
we want to put around our responses to students:

1   *Questions should align with the instructional goal (standard).* There are
    lots of good questions, but there are only a few questions
    that are appropriate for any given standard. If you need to
    assess your students' comprehension of a particular author's
    perspective about slavery, for instance, asking questions
    about the role of the Constitution in enabling the slave

trade is probably a little off task (unless the author in question is using the Constitution as part of their argument). Questions should be laser focused on the standard and associated local summative assessment.

2 *Feedback should be about content accuracy and disciplinary ways of structuring ideas, not language accuracy and content summary.* Without a doubt, it is difficult not to edit our students' papers. (Trust us, we fight this urge every day.) Such line-by-line editing, though, should be reserved for larger assignments, in which editing is the final stage. More often with formative assessments, the goal is to make sure that the students are expressing the content appropriately, demonstrating their understanding within the discipline. Is there a bit of language correction that might occur as part of this process? Yes—helping students to code-switch to academic ways of speaking and writing is important. Should we correct every spelling and punctuation mistake? No—doing so misses the point of formative assessment and overwhelms the students with "marks." It deemphasizes the content understanding we are trying to teach and assess.

3 *There is no answer that is so perfect that it can't be improved.* With any luck, you will have created an appropriately scaffolded learning segment that really helps all students to do a fantastic job on their local summative assessment. They may all score the highest possible score on the assessment! That is an excellent goal. But even if they do, your students' work can still be improved upon. For all students, institute a "glows" and "grows" approach to formative assessment feedback. On each student's work, indicate what the student did well (glows) and what they could do to improve the work in the future (grows). Maybe the student could elaborate more on

a specific topic, use more connecting words to build complex sentences, or reduce the number of words used by using more abstract nominal groups (e.g., "the colonists" instead of "the people who lived in the colonies").

What to do with the formative assessment analysis. As you analyze students' work or hold discussions with your students, you will be able to identify strengths and weaknesses within your students' learning. It is this insight that should drive your planning and delivery of instruction. It may be that you find a particular area of weakness across the class that will require reteaching with the incorporation of different instructional strategies. You might find areas of strength that suggest a deeper dive into the content than you had first intended. As you discover the patterns of what is working and what is not, your instructional approaches should be reflective of the learning already taking place in your class. Chapter 7 will provide a more in-depth discussion of your use of postassessment data.

Summative Assessments: Measuring Students' Mastery

In chapter 2, we detailed a taxonomy of assessments from formative local assessments to standardized assessments. Your formative local assessments (your checks for understanding, student work samples, exit slips, etc.) form the basis for the work your students will do in the summative local assessment. It would be strange for a student to do poorly on all of the checks for understanding but well on the summative local assessment, and vice versa. Unlike district, state, and national-level standardized assessments, formative and summative local assessments are teacher created, known in advance of instruction, and contextualized to the learning that is

happening in the classroom. Whereas decontextualized standardized assessments might assess students' knowledge and
skills differently from the context of the class, formative and
summative local assessments are born from the class.

This synergy between formative and summative local
assessments is the "black box" of learning (Black & Wiliam,
1998). The data that teachers generate when they intentionally
and thoughtfully assess students' understandings and skills
can pinpoint the areas of relative strength and weakness that
any one student has on any given subject matter. These data
can be collected to provide a broader picture of the students
in the class, demonstrating their capacities as influenced by
teacher instruction. These moment-by-moment data allow
teachers to see into their students' learning much like a plane's
"black box" monitors moment-by-moment systems, providing critical information about what worked and what didn't.

LANDMARK

When you planned your learning segment, we recommended (as do your
education professors and most curriculum scholars) that you "begin with
the end in mind." That is, we recommended that you develop a summative
assessment for the end of your learning segment (aligned with your standard) that would serve as a measure of your students' abilities to incorporate what they learned across the learning segment in a single assignment.
This process is called "backward design" (Wiggins & McTighe, 2005), and it is
considered best practice in curriculum development. Engaging this process
allows you to "teach to the test" in the best possible ways because (1) you
created the test (in this case an authentic assessment, not a traditional test),
(2) the "test" is aligned to the curricular standard (which the field agrees is
an important thing for students to learn), and (3) the "test" is a product of
your own instruction (which will highlight what students directly learned

from your learning segment). If your "test" is fair and well aligned, teaching to the test is a great opportunity to assess students' learning and growth (Gallagher, 2009).

The summative assessment that your students complete at the end of the learning segment is a culmination of their moment-by-moment work in class. In that cumulative sense, summative local assessments demonstrate a finality of a learning experience—that of your learning segment. But these assessments are also formative in the grander picture of your course. You will use those data from the summative local assessments to make adjustments to your future instruction, particularly instruction toward the guiding standard of your learning segment. Remember, the guiding standard of your learning segment is something to be mastered over a greater period of time. The data garnered for that standard in one learning segment can and should be used to plan for another learning segment that continues to build on students' competencies in relation to the standard.

This process of reexposing, reteaching, and reassessing students on a particular standard is crucial. Assessment studies in the early 1990s found that as students and teachers prepared for and took the same standardized test for multiple years, test scores rose for about five years total. After that time, test scores plateaued or flattened slightly. A new test would be implemented, and although the initial test scores would be low, they would rise over the next couple of years. In these latter years, when students and teachers got good at the test, the state could claim that "everyone was above average"—a phenomenon known as the Lake Wobegon Effect (Cannell,

1987; Koretz, 1988), named after the fictional Minnesota town "where all the women are strong, all the men are good looking, *and all the children are above average*" (Oxford Reference, n.d., emphasis added). Since the tests focused on standards, the rise in scores was due to the students performing better on those particular standards; the rise in scores did not mean that the students were doing better all around (Linn, 1994).

As students practice standards-aligned assessments, they will get better at meeting the requirements of those standards. You may have experienced this yourself if you have taken a standardized test, such as the SAT or Praxis, multiple times. Crucial to this particular process of formative local and summative local assessment work are the variables outside the context of the specific standard. The content of the assessment, the genre of the assessment, the teacher's instruction around the assessment, and the assessment criteria (thinking about the developmental aspects of assessment creation) all play a role in students' success—along with myriad other educational issues. Revisiting standards with varied authentic assessments provides a truer picture of a student's proficiency than does a repeated assessment or a one-and-done assessment.

There are some things that you can do throughout your learning segment, however, that will enable your students to successfully build their capacities to engage instructional standards in different contexts (e.g., with different content or developmental academic language expectations). The most important thing for you to do is to recenter the focus of the assessment onto the student (Kulasegaram & Rangachari, 2018). Even summative assessments are part of the learning process; effective teachers will be able to harness the learning activity housed within the assessment itself and use it to deepen students' understanding. Focusing your assessment on your students and their continued growth as learners will be much easier to do when you move away from what many people consider traditional "tests."

Historically, tests have been measures of factual recall. Though research abounds demonstrating that these types of assessments do little to improve students' learning, or to truly measure the students' mastery that they intend, they are still largely used in academic settings. One reason for this persistence is the relative ease and low cost with which these assessments can be produced (Kulasegaram & Rangachari, 2018). They are also relatively objective, which aids in their administration and scoring. What these tests end up promoting, however, is a "gorge and purge" mentality in your students; many students will study the factual information assessed on these tests, committing it to memory, only to purge it from their memories immediately following the test. In their minds, there is a disconnect between the assessment and the true reason for learning. They believe they only need to remember these facts long enough to pass the test.

Problem-based learning (PBL). You need to design assessments to measure students' learning, but you should avoid using traditional multiple-choice-type formats. What do you do instead? Problem-based learning is a possible solution. When you engage your students in PBL, your role shifts from the "sage on the stage" to facilitator of learning. The learning that your students engage in also shifts from "gorge and purge" factual recall to problem solving and critical thinking.

Though the PBL pedagogy is one of the strongest educational approaches today, its roots can be traced back to John Dewey's philosophies over a century ago (Delisle, 1997). Dewey argued for the emphasis in the classroom to be placed on the "doing" rather than on the "learning"; in his view, the act of doing would demand that students make connections and think critically, therefore, naturally leading to the learning intended by the teacher. Problem-based learning was first used in medical classrooms for this specific purpose. The focus on textbook learning and lecture did not allow students to easily apply their learning to new experiences and contexts. When PBL was used, students began learning to solve medical problems rather than memorizing basic medical information. Our intended change in the secondary classroom follows this model.

There are several defining features of problem-based learning: (1) the work surrounds a challenging and realistic problem to be overcome; (2) the students are afforded the opportunity to make critical decisions and take ownership of their learning experiences; (3) the students work cooperatively, building their interpersonal and management skills; and (4) the work culminates in authentic demonstrations of students' skill (De Graaff & Kolmos, 2003). Using this pedagogical approach will lend itself to an authentic assessment of skill. Proposing a problem to your students will often suggest an appropriate assessment to be used. For example, consider tasking your students with the following problem: "The subway station is going to be improved at a cost of $5 million. By law, 2 percent of this money is to be devoted to public art in the station. You are members of a committee that has two tasks. The first is to set up the rules and regulations for artists who wish to submit entries. The second is to determine the criteria or guidelines for selecting the winning designs" (Delisle, 1997). In reading this sample problem, it should become apparent to you that the students are being challenged to formulate a set of submission rules and scoring guidelines for hypothetical local artists. As the teacher, you will be using this final product as your assessment. Having a scoring rubric for a project of this type will be very helpful in allowing you to determine to what extent your students met your intended objectives.

Because of the nature of the problems and projects associated with PBL, you may end up with a multitude of assessment formats, such as presentations, videos, lists, letters, plans of action, posters, and more. These activities are generally tied to the wording of the problem you propose to your class. Another option for authentic assessment is the use of mind maps. Mind maps are colorful, image-heavy, nonlinear representations of students' knowledge (Zvauya, Purandare, Young, & Pallan, 2017). These assessment pieces allow students to both build and demonstrate their understanding through creative, student-centered, metacognitive means. You may also consider using a portfolio approach to assessment, in which students build and collect artifacts throughout the learning segment to demonstrate their acquired skills and knowledge.

SCENIC DETOUR

The Role of Standardized Assessments in Teaching and Learning

Standardized tests have a bad reputation among parents and teachers alike. There certainly are some negative aspects of these tests, such as students' anxiety and unfair teacher evaluations based on test-score data, but the idea behind standardized tests is not inherently bad. These tests have been around for decades and were originally designed to measure students' progress on a large scale. The fact that they are "standardized" means that students in different places are all exposed to the same sets of questions, making comparisons between and among student groups plausible.

Critiquing the use of standardized tests is beyond the scope of this book; however, there is one main point you should consider based on what you have learned about assessment. There are certainly flaws in the development and use of standardized tests, but there are often-overlooked benefits as well. If standardized tests are based on the standards, and we are in agreement that the standards are what students need to know to be successful, the tests should measure how well the students can or cannot meet those standards. You will inevitably hear teachers complaining that all they ever have time to do is to "teach to the test." Teaching to the test should mean teaching to the standards. It is what you are meant to do as long as you are doing so in a student-centered, pedagogically effective way.

Preferencing Disciplinary, Authentic Assessment

We have spent a great deal of time discussing the use of authentic assessment, even (and especially) for summative data. As a profession, we continue to move away from the rote memorization and factual recall associated with traditional assessment formats such as the multiple-choice, fill-in-the-blank, or matching tests and quizzes used for many generations. This shift away from lower levels of thinking leads to advances in critical-thinking and problem-solving abilities in our students (Bruner, 1986; Robinson, 2011; Vygotsky, 1978; Wagner, 2012; Wineburg, 2018). The cognitive processes used in such problem-based explorations are not as easily measured with the older assessment formats; a multiple-choice quiz leaves little room for students' creativity, innovation, and autonomy. If these higher-order thinking processes are the goal of our instruction, our assessments must be designed to measure them.

To truly understand what knowledge and skills your students have gained, you must create authentic assessment opportunities in which they can demonstrate their creative, problem-solving abilities. Let's return to our original starting point: the standard. Most standards are designed and referred to as "indicators" or "performance expectations," which are already phrased in a way that implies the appropriate assessment type. For example, the standards may demand that the students explain, develop a model, compare and contrast, or design an investigation. Some of these demands (develop a model, design an investigation) are more specific than others (explain, compare and contrast). For the more specific expectations, your assessment should be the model or plan for investigation called for within the standard. There is some inherent flexibility even in these expectations, however. Developing a model of some concept could be accomplished in a two-dimensional drawing with labeled components of a system, or it could be a three-dimensional model made from a multitude of supplies. Some teachers (or students) may even choose to model concepts virtually through the assistance of technology. You may decide which of these methods is best for your class, or you may allow your students to choose for themselves. The less specific standards (explain, describe, compare) allow you to approach the assessment in many ways; you simply need to identify which of your options is best for your particular students and the concept you are teaching. For example, you may have students explain a concept through an oral presentation to the class, through a journaling activity shared only with you, as an essay, or in a discussion among students. It would be inappropriate, however, when your students are charged with explaining or modeling a concept that you give the students a quiz in which they are tasked with matching words to definitions.

Once you have chosen your authentic assessment, one that will actually measure the capacities you aim to build in your students, you will be able to gather better data (and therefore a more accurate understanding) of what your students have learned. These types of assessments are also the preference of the edTPA and teaching profession because they allow you to give better feedback to your students, promoting further learning. With a multiple-choice test, it is much more difficult for you to identify the thinking process used by each of your students; sometimes, they just make a guess! Your feedback to them on such an assessment would usually be the indication of the correct letter choice. This interaction pattern between student and teacher does little to address misconceptions and allow for growth. With an authentic assessment, such as a performance, model, investigation, or written composition, you are able to follow more closely the thinking process each student took to produce the culminating assignment. You can catch mistakes that are being made and clarify misconceptions. You will have a better understanding of your students as learners, *and* they will be better able to learn from their own work.

Summary

Assessment is just as important to teaching and learning as the actual planning and delivery of instruction are. You will be using your assessments for two main purposes: to evaluate students' progress and to evaluate students' mastery. Each of these assessments will need to be aligned to your learning goals or objectives, which in turn are based on the standards. Additionally, these assessments will need to be authentic in scope, actually measuring your students' capacities toward the specific goal of your learning segment. Planning and using these assessments effectively will allow for deeper learning for all of your students.

ORIENTATION

Where Are You Now?

1 How are formative and summative assessments different? How do these differences affect the ways in which they are used in the classroom?

2 Describe two of the most memorable assessments you had to take as a student. Why do you remember them so well? How did they deepen (or confuse) your understanding of the subject matter?

3 Research what standardized test(s) are used in your district or state. How do these assessments affect the students and teachers?

CHAPTER 4

Planning to Support Students

ORIENTATION
You Are Here

You now have an understanding of planning for instruction; a clear alignment connecting the standards to your objective and assessment will allow for a more authentic learning experience for your students. The way you design instruction ultimately impacts how your students will engage the material presented. You may be starting to work with your cooperating teacher, in some capacity, to build these types of instructional units, or you may be practicing this process through your coursework. Ultimately, you will want to practice this process independently and ask your cooperating teacher or professor to oversee your efforts.

This chapter will teach you to approach the planning process with the students in mind. Once you know *what* needs to be taught, you will begin to consider *how* to teach it. This process will be directly based on the unique characteristics of the learners within your class as well as the class as a whole.

Beginning with Students in Mind

You may have noticed that we haven't said much about your students yet. This was by design. Most of what you have read to this point relates explicitly to the instructional design courses you probably took throughout your teacher preparation program. The previous chapters explained those instructional design components in terms of the edTPA language. Understanding that language will help you to make better decisions about the structure and content of your learning segments.

Critical to all of this, though, are your students. Just as we have designed this book with your experiences, strengths, weaknesses, comforts, and anxieties in mind, so too must you attend to your students' abilities, contexts, and interests. Attending to these factors increases students' self-efficacy, which can increase student learning to an effect size of 0.70, and teacher credibility with students, which has an effect size of 0.90 on student learning, as it increases students' view of teachers as trustworthy and caring (Hattie, 2011). Designing instruction with your students in mind is key to increasing student learning.

The conceptual underpinnings of the edTPA show preference for constructivist approaches to selecting instructional materials and strategies. Constructivist approaches call you to use particular modes of teaching and learning that require an understanding of your students as holistic learners. Understanding these aspects, what they require you to know about your students and how they impact instructional decision-making, is critical, then, to good planning and to strong implementation.

The Myth of Average

Todd Rose (2015) tells a story of the United States Air Force in 1952. In this post–World War II era, the United States was engaged in the Cold War with the Soviet Union. On both sides, military might and ability were being used for war-footed posturing. But the United States Air Force had a problem. Even though it was spending top dollar on the most advanced fighter jets and training highly qualified pilots, it was getting worse results against simulated Soviet pilots.

When cockpits were first created in the 1920s, designers built them to fit the dimensions of the average male pilot (women were not considered at that time). As planes flew faster and farther, and as the technology in those planes became more complex, the rightness-to-fit between the plane and pilot became critical for mission success—and pilot survival. In a study commissioned by the Air Force, four thousand pilots were measured along ten dimensions. Exactly zero of the pilots fit the average dimensions. The planes were literally designed for no human being!

It wasn't until the Air Force forced manufacturers to develop new technologies that allowed for adjustable cockpit features (like the adjustable seats and steering wheels we have in cars today) that the pilots were able to perform better. Those features now allowed the United States to recruit the best pilots, not just the ones that fit best in our planes.

As you begin considering potential learning segments to include in your edTPA portfolios, you may be focusing on the standards and content to be taught, disassociated from the students in the classroom. That doesn't mean that you are planning incorrectly; it simply means you are planning incompletely. Planning your content first only becomes inappropriate when you fail to factor in the variety of your students—when you expect all of your pilots to fit into the same cockpit.

Constructivism

While the behaviors that students exhibit related to mastery objectives are important, they are only a product of the real work students do individually and collectively in the classroom. This idea that thinking and understanding are both an individual and collective process is critical to understanding not only how we human beings learn but also what the edTPA expects you to demonstrate. Both rely on a definition of *constructivism* that represents the link between *cognitivism* and *culture* in the learning process (Aubrey & Riley, 2019).

To understand this link, let's explore an example that Jerome Bruner, the godfather of constructivism, provides to explain this process.

> The concept of prime numbers appears to be more readily grasped when the child, through construction, discovers that certain handfuls of beans cannot be laid out in completed rows and columns. Such quantities have either to be laid out in a single file or in an incomplete row-column design in which there is always one extra or one too few to fill the pattern. These patterns, the child learns, happen to be called prime. It is easy for the child to go from this step to the recognition that a multiple table, so called, is a record sheet of quantities in completed multiple rows and columns. Here is factoring, multiplication and primes in a construction that can be visualized. (Culatta, 2020)

When we give our children M&Ms, one of the first things they often do is to organize them by color and count them. Children (and most adults) are actually fascinated with numbers and how things can be counted, categorized, and arranged. They are even interested in understanding universal principles that are related to the physical world, even if those principles appear to have no direct bearing on their lives. So how is it that we can help students to construct their knowledge of abstract concepts (e.g., addition and multiplication tables) that they have been told are boring and useless?

In the preceding example, Bruner (1973) describes a process that has three essential elements for composing a constructivist lesson. First, the instruction is based on an experience through which students are willing and able to learn. In a low-risk environment, giving students something to count and organize will allow them to notice properties of the activity. Many children have probably had similar experiences in their own lives. For example, Jason's children count their peas at the dinner table rather than eating them—they have lots of experience! Given our students' prior experiences, and their fascination with organizing manipulatives, our students are primed (no pun intended) to play with the concepts of such a lesson.

The second element of the constructivist lesson described in Bruner's example, though Bruner doesn't explicitly discuss it, is the careful design of instruction that would allow the students to easily grasp the concepts. Providing students with various sets of beans that allow them to find numbers that are ill fit for the row-column design allows them to start identifying these sets. Through just a naming process, then, students can learn that these numbers are called prime, and they can explore the patterns of these numbers and compare them with other numbers. As a teacher, it is your job to carefully plan your lessons (choosing the right number of beans to provide to students) to make the learning objective clear and attainable.

The final element in the bean-counting activity relates to the application of the learning in the lesson to external and increasingly abstract contexts. The patterns students use in the

classroom activity can be used to extrapolate beyond counting beans to more abstract mathematical concepts (factoring,
multiplication, and primes). Since the students constructed
their understanding of prime numbers and were able to
explore the relationships between and among those numbers,
they are prepared for more abstract representations ("modes,"
in Bruner's terminology) of extended mathematical concepts.

   **SCALE: When repeated throughout units of instruction, such a con-
structivist approach allows you to engage your students in two ways
that the edTPA finds critically important: (1) personal, cultural, and
community assets and (2) prior academic learning.** These aspects
of planning design, repeated throughout Tasks 1 and 2, are
related to discussions of "knowledge of students." Since a constructivist approach to instruction requires an understanding
of the individual student as well as the class, it makes sense
that the group's assets (both inside and outside the school) as
well as their prior academic knowledge would play a key role
in instructional design.

Student Assets

Students bring assets into the classroom. Their experiences,
preferences, and passions help to build a cohesive classroom
environment as well as to expand the class's ways of knowing (its epistemological stances). These assets can be personal
(with an emphasis on particular interests), cultural (with an
emphasis on traditions, languages, and environments), or
based in community (with an emphasis on common experiences and knowledge from the surrounding area) in nature.*
Each student brings an amalgamation of assets to the classroom environment (Johnson, 2005). Some of these assets are

---

* For the edTPA definition of *asset*, please see your handbook's glossary.

individual to the student, while some are shared across many students. Still other assets have easily transferable values (e.g., lessons from major world religions). Constructivist planning invites teachers to tap into any and all of these assets to connect lesson activities to students' lived experiences (Fosnot, 2005).

In Bruner's example, for instance, the teacher tapped into the personal assets of the students' interest in counting and organizing manipulatable items—in this case, beans. But the teacher could have extended this connection further. What if the teacher knew that the students enjoyed marshmallows? Or, seeing that it was nearing Halloween (in areas where it is celebrated), the teacher had the students count small candies? Here, the activities are not only aligned to the students' developmental level(s) but are also tied to the teacher's knowledge of the students' personal preference assets and cultural assets (Halloween celebrations).

The key to success in this particular area of planning (and in your resulting edTPA portfolio) is to clearly and purposefully connect what you know of your students' personal, cultural, and community assets with the activities you plan in the classroom. It is not enough to simply list out observations of your students in a written commentary or to make superficial connections between the assets and your planning. Instead, take some time getting to know your students. Use what you know about them to plan your instruction. Then, provide a full description of why your choices were made.

Prior Academic Learning

When we think about *prior academic learning* as the edTPA defines it, it is often useful to think about the term *prior knowledge*. Though there are many definitions of *prior knowledge*, a strong middle-ground definition comes from Harm Biemans and P. R. Simons (1996), who view prior knowledge as "all knowledge learners have when entering a learning environment that is potentially relevant for acquiring new knowledge" (p. 163). We have known for quite some time that students' minds are not blank slates (tabula rasa) and that they enter all settings with preconceived notions and knowledge of the world. To the extent that these notions are correct, teachers can use them to develop new background knowledge (as in Bruner's example). To the extent that these notions are incorrect, however, teachers need to engage students to address misconceptions.

Whereas brainstorming, discussion, and diagnostic assessment techniques can help to identify students' correct and incorrect prior knowledge, addressing misconceptions and building on students' prior knowledge can be difficult because such knowledge is not discrete. In other words, the prior knowledge that any one student has is not isolated in their brain. Rather, any relevant information (see Biemans and Simon's definition) is situated in a network with all of the other information that that student has.

A way of visualizing this process is through Walter Kintsch's (1998) model of comprehension, in which the brain breaks a text into small ideas (propositions) and then those ideas are reconfigured into the reader's prior knowledge. This reconfiguration is what is remembered in the reader's mental representation of the ideas of the text. By understanding the ways that words are folded into the networked structure of information, we can begin to understand the ways that information is interpreted (and misinterpreted). Information, in this case *words*, travel through a process of representation and then through at least two networks (systems) of comprehension before they are integrated into the experiential (situation) model of a person's understanding.

Let's say, for example, that you are visiting a new city and you are examining a subway map, thinking about the best ways to get to all of the city's tourist sites. On this simple map, there is an array of words (names of stations and tourist sites), colors (associated with lines on the map), and circles of various sizes (associated with the stations, especially where they intersect with the colored lines on the page). The first step of integration is understanding the individual words and symbols on the page. This involves decoding the words and recognizing some of the place names. You will also understand the colors on the lines to indicate various subway routes and the circles to represent the stations. This is the "linguistic representation" of the integration.

Next, your brain will try to make sense of the map as a text, that is, as a whole document. You will recognize not only individual places and subway lines but also how they interact as a system. This system involves which lines connect to which other lines as well as which lines allow passengers to get closest to their desired destinations. As your goal is to see specific sites as well as to be as efficient in your travel as possible, this systems-level understanding is important to understanding the map as a text.

But you don't understand the map in isolation. You understand the map through the filter of your experiences with maps, subway systems, and transportation in general. Maybe you used to live in a city and remember how crowded (and confusing) large stations can be. Or maybe you have never been on a subway before and are a bit nervous; your travel trepidation might lead you to understanding the map in terms of the fewest transfers possible, even if the route is less efficient overall. It is at this stage that your experiences (prior knowledge) and the text of the map integrate. You will remember salient details of the map related to those experiences and, with some degree of comfort, be able to navigate the system. But your navigation is via an integrated model in which your prior knowledge and your new text-based knowledge are integrated.

Our prior knowledge and experiences prevent us from comprehending information in isolation, which means that we don't all comprehend information in the same way, even when we are reading the same text. The students in your class will have had different experiences in their lives, meaning that your students' prior knowledge will inevitably be very varied. For example, some students have very involved families that provide support in homework and take the children to visit museums and nature centers. Other students may have limited adult support at home, or they may unfortunately *be* the support at home, taking care of younger siblings while a parent works. Some students will have traveled to other countries, while other students may have scarcely left the town they were born in. Thus, every person's prior knowledge is slightly different, making it difficult for a novice teacher to incorporate this collective prior knowledge in a lesson. Even if you could, there would be a wide range that you would have to accommodate for.

This is where the distinction between prior knowledge and prior academic learning becomes very important. It was necessary to review how prior knowledge is constructed as it relates to prior academic learning. As a teacher, it will be the prior academic learning, however, that you will use to build your lessons. You can't control those outside experiences that your students bring to the classroom; what you can control is the academic learning that takes place before a learning segment. You can do this in two ways: by taking the time to understand what was explicitly taught to the students in the past or by pre-teaching important content yourself so that you know all of the students will bring a certain level of prior learning to the learning segment you plan to teach.

Prior to teaching a learning segment, it is critical to know not only what students have been taught in the past but what they have learned (those are two different things) *and* how confident they feel about their learning. This information should be gathered from the curriculum, from prior assessments, and from continuous communication with your students. These three sources will allow you to build an effective learning segment tailored to your students' prior academic learning.

Information gathered from the curriculum is important because it allows you to see the scope and sequence of learning. For example, in New Jersey, students should explicitly learn about George Washington three times throughout their schooling career. If the curriculum indicates that your class is the students' first exposure to Washington and the colonial period, then your expectations of your students' prior academic learning should be limited and based solely on students' out-of-school knowledge. Your expectations should shift if students are engaging the material for the third time. Notice that your expectations *should* shift, but they might not. Information based on curriculum alone is the weakest of the three sources of information just mentioned because it assumes that what is in the curriculum is actually taught (challenge 1), what is taught is taught well (challenge 2), and what is taught well is remembered by the students (challenge 3). A fourth challenge is to consider that not all of the students in your class have experienced the same curriculum, teachers, and/or levels of instruction. Studies of schooling in the United States show rather large variations in between-school and within-school performance (Sahlberg, 2014), which lead to variation in students' prior academic learning.

Assessment information should also be used to build your learning segment. Many teachers rely on standardized assessments, especially at the beginning of a school year, to understand students' prior academic learning. These are not always useful because many are norm-referenced, meaning that the assessments compare the students in your class to large samples but tell little about how the students in the class compare to one another. For the purposes of instruction planning, criterion-referenced standardized assessments are better. Criterion-referenced assessments say something about what an individual student can do related to a particular task/standard, something that is useful for developing mastery objectives and for thinking about the curricular assets that each student brings to the class.

Even better than standardized assessments, though, are local formative assessments. Standards-based and qualitative in nature, these assessments allow teachers to see the thinking behind the product—to peek into the students' thought processes (Black & Wiliam, 1998). Through these assessments, teachers can identify misconceptions, links between content-area facts, and abilities to produce products in particular genres (e.g., compare and contrast). These three areas can be consistently assessed via various checks for understanding (CfU) throughout the lessons prior to the learning segment.

Just as critical as these assessments, though, is continuous communication with the students. In our experience, this is the aspect of learning-segment design that student teachers miss the most. While the aforementioned types of data are important, understanding the ways in which students learn best and how they feel about their own knowledge and skills (their self-efficacy around the learning that happens in your classroom) is critical to impactful instruction. If students have high self-efficacy about their learning, the effect size of that learning is 0.7 (Hattie, 2011), meaning that the learning that happens in such a context can really move students' learning forward. Understanding how your students feel about their learning, what they are confident about, and where they are a little insecure is no small thing. Learn about your students in this way and be sure to share these insights in your teacher performance assessment commentary.

Together, curricular information, assessment information, and student self-efficacy information will enable you to build stronger learning segments by activating prior academic learning. When the best teachers are able to leverage students' prior knowledge (which includes academic learning), they can move a class more than one year forward in their instruction (Hattie, 2011). The better you understand your students' prior academic learning and use it in your instruction, the more effective you will be as a teacher.

PLANNING PATHWAYS

Explore the data your cooperating teacher has on students' prior standardized and diagnostic assessments. Survey your class about their interests, knowledge, and self-efficacy. Take a walk through the neighborhoods around your school. Then, create a one-page summary of your target class on the basis of these data and relate your understanding to an upcoming unit.

Implementing Constructivist Pedagogies

The edTPA's preference for constructivism can be found throughout the handbook language. The Task 1 rubrics explicitly mention lessons that *build on each other, meaningful contexts, supports* for students, *prior academic learning,* and *multiple forms of assessment.* Task 2 rubrics continue these themes from Task 1, adding *challenging learning environment* and *building on students' responses* as interactive tasks during teaching. Task 3's focus on feedback and learning patterns is also consistent with constructivism. Constructivist theory, as described earlier, is woven throughout the handbook.

But as anyone who has taught knows, implementing constructivist pedagogies is not easy. Even with a good understanding of students' prior academic learning, their personal, cultural, and community assets, and professional pedagogical content knowledge, designing instruction to meet all students' needs can be challenging. What is not discussed in the handbook is how to design instruction; fortunately, this is a skill that you learned in your teacher preparation program.

In the following sections, we review two design methods that we have found particularly helpful for designing support for student learning. Both design methods draw on a deep literature while also acknowledging the persistence of technology in education; they are old design methods for new educational contexts that include digital technology and shifting student demographics. Using your understanding of your students, Universal Design and Culturally Responsive approaches to instructional design will help you support all students in your class.

Universal Design for Learning (UDL)

In the very first task of the edTPA, you will be asked to describe all of your students who (1) have an Individualized Education Program (IEP) or 504, (2) have specific language needs (e.g., your ELL students), and/or (3) are struggling students. Many candidates that we have worked with simply insert required accommodations into their lesson plans, assuring that they are supporting student learning by applying what is needed for specific students to succeed in given activities. This meets the letter of the law. But we also know that when we design instruction to the edges of our students' capabilities, those accommodations support student learning across the class (Meyer, Rose, & Gordon, 2016).

Universal Design for Learning (UDL) is an instructional design model that encourages teachers to develop varied modes of (1) representations, (2) expression, and (3) engagement for student learning (Meyer et al., 2016). By providing students with reasonable options to interact with a variety of texts, create products of their own learning, and engage with the teacher, their classmates, and the world, teachers can accommodate a range of learners without pigeonholing the terms *accommodation* and *inclusion* into narrow special education contexts.

To use our ecosystem example from chapter 2, a teacher could enable students to interact along these different modes of learning throughout a learning segment. If the local summative assessment for the learning segment was for students to develop a model to describe the flow of energy and matter within an ecosystem, a teacher could provide a number of options for how the topic is explored, how students interact with the materials and each other, and how they demonstrate their learning.

Notice in figure 4.1 that all of the ways that information can be represented, expressed, and engaged are disciplinarily appropriate for a science classroom. While there is a lot to be said for interdisciplinary modes of expression, for the edTPA, you are demonstrating the ways in which students engage in disciplinary ways of thinking. Adopting a UDL model enables students to select options for their instruction that fit best with their ways of thinking while at the same time situating

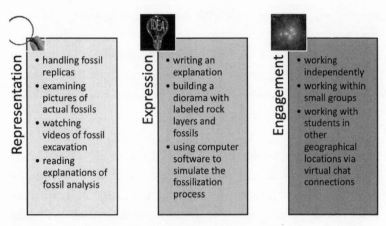

Figure 4.1. Example of disciplinary thinking behind UDL model

the learning in the discipline. Using concept rubrics, then, the teacher can assess student learning, gaining insights into each student's learning and across the class as a whole. The ways that things can be learned doesn't need to be the same for all of the students, even if we want all of the students to learn the same thing!

Employing a UDL model requires teachers to really know their students. Using what you know from their IEPs, 504s, language assessments, and diagnostic test scores is a good starting point. You may also want to survey your students to find out how they like to learn best, what they like best about school, and what other creative talents they have. Such information is useful for you to select appropriate modes of representation, expression, and engagement that really fit with your students' needs and strengths. Providing these options, in addition to fulfilling additional accommodation obligations, can make the learning more enjoyable for everyone and allow you to engage in the disciplinary, constructivist conversations you want with your students.

Culturally Responsive Pedagogies

The UDL model allows us to be mindful of students' differing learning profiles. In a similar way, Culturally Responsive Pedagogies (CRPs) allow us to be mindful of students' differing culture profiles. Just as students bring different learning needs, expectations, and assets to the classroom, these students also bring differing cultural needs, expectations, and assets. By highlighting culture, however, CRPs seek to engage students in the "co-construction of knowledge through the use of cultural knowledge, prior experiences, frames of reference, and performance styles" (Gay, 2000, p. 31). CRPs, then, provide teachers with another lens to look through when developing student-responsive instruction.

This lens allows teachers to look critically at their curriculum and instructional materials, identifying who is represented (or valued) within the curriculum. With this information, teachers can intentionally select topics, texts, and classroom materials that reduce stereotypes between students, between teachers and students, and between students and the curriculum. Such a lens encourages teachers to be intentionally inclusive of all students in relation to social characteristics that have historically been underprivileged (e.g., race, language, ethnicity, and sex) (Johnson, 2005).

A long literature of critical education has documented that the traditional classroom curriculum focuses on groups that are historically privileged (Apple, 1996, 2000; Banks & Banks, 2010; FitzGerald, 1979; Freire, 1970; Giroux, 1995; Hollie, 2018; Johnson, 2005). Textbooks often reference, cite, and value heterosexual, White, middle-/upper-class, male perspectives. Other, less privileged groups are added into the curriculum but are not featured in a central role. Thus, when we ask students of diverse backgrounds to imagine themselves as scientists or dancers or authors or *whatever*, many are left without role models. This lack of role models is not a function of a lack of African American, female mathematicians, for example, but a function of curricular decisions not to discuss their work. CRPs encourage teachers to intentionally consider these stereotypes and provide instruction that values students' cultural and linguistic backgrounds as well as diverse backgrounds found in society. This is *additive schooling* in contrast to the *subtractive schooling* that Angela Valenzuela (1999) found in her study of schooling and curriculum.

One useful way for thinking about implementing CRPs in the classroom is through Sharroky Hollie's (2018) VABB model. With your students in mind, instruction should (1) validate, (2) affirm, (3) build, and (4) bridge the cultures of the students in the class *as well as* cultures not in the class that are equally a part of society. When the edTPA asks you to take your students' personal, cultural, and community assets into account, these are the pieces that it is referencing.

Implementing CRPs looks different for various contexts, but there are some similarities that we might see across different people's learning segments. Literacy lessons might include texts written by authors or featuring *main* characters of diverse cultures. Science lessons might highlight the work of historical and/or modern scientists who represent historically underrepresented cultures. History lessons might directly challenge the White, male narrative of U.S. history. Math lessons might include a short minilesson on the non-Western development of many algebraic methods. All of these subject areas could engage students with modern data and texts from relevant newspapers and magazines, exposing students to the diverse array of literary, scientific, and social science writers we are fortunate to have in the world.

Obviously, these are only examples and do not come anywhere close to the depth and breadth that one could take Culturally Responsive Pedagogies. What is critical here is that you (1) know your students and the cultures and communities to which they belong, (2) recognize that most curricula are tailored to the "typical" students (read: White, male, middle class, heterosexual), and (3) provide consistent chances for students to engage in Hollie's (2018) VABB model. Your learning segment will only feature a brief episode of such work but should be a window into the typical, culturally inclusive environment you have cultivated.

Summary

When we plan supports for students, we need to think about the specific students in our classrooms. Planning to the average—be that for fighter pilots or for students in a classroom—creates a plan for no one. As discussed in this chapter, all students need supports if we are engaging them in progressively more rigorous instruction. These supports might look different for each student, so thinking about how a Universal Design for Learning (UDL) model might allow students to engage with material in different ways is critical to designing flexible instruction.

We also have to remember, though, that the students in our classes are diverse—even if they "look" the same. Students bring different cultural assets to our classrooms, and those assets can be used to expand and deepen relationships and learning across the class. Learning content is important, but you have the ability and duty to define, expand, and challenge traditional content structures, an ability that simultaneously allows you to connect with your students and help your students connect with the content. Layering Culturally

Responsive Pedagogies with UDL principles creates opportunities for powerful instruction.

Where Are You Now?

1 What experiences have you had with the term *constructivism*? Has it been related to *hands-on learning*? In what ways are the two terms related and unrelated?

2 Plan a one-page summary of the assets and prior academic learning for two different classes you teach/observe or have taught/observed in the past. In what ways do these summaries challenge you to create different instructional experiences for your students?

3 Choose one of your own lesson plans (or one from your cooperating teacher). Reframe it using a UDL model. What assumptions were made in the original lesson that are challenged by using the UDL model?

4 Using the class textbook, district curriculum, or supplemental texts available in your field placement, explore the variety of social characteristics represented. Which groups are most privileged in the text(s)? How do these characteristics realistically compare to those represented in your class of students?

5 What do your students care about? (Actually ask them!) Explain why they should care about what you are teaching them this week. If you do not see any direct connections between their personal interests and your learning segment, add those connections for your students.

CHAPTER 5

Understanding and Using Academic Language

You Are Here

On the basis of your learning over the previous chapters, you are probably becoming more comfortable, or at least more practiced, in planning learning segments and assessments based on the students in your class. Better planning for instruction is dependent on your ability to plan meaningful assessments and to tailor these assessments toward your unique and diverse students. The content you plan to teach and assess, however, is only one side of the story. The language used within your discipline to communicate this content is the counterpart and will require equally careful planning and support.

This chapter will explore how to approach the academic language of authentic, disciplinary assessments and the lessons that support student practice toward these goals. Some of the terms in this chapter might be new to you; the academic language terms that the edTPA uses come from linguistics research, not literacy research. Once understood, though, the ways in which *academic language* is conceptualized in the edTPA will

be clear and will help you to structure both your learning segment and your assessments.

What Is Academic Language?

As your students progress in their schooling, they are apprenticed in an increasingly content-specific set of language demands. These demands take students from contextualized everyday language to more decontextualized language we call *disciplinary* or *academic language* (Christie & Martin, 2007; Fang & Schleppegrell, 2010; Larsson, 2018; Schleppegrell, 2004). Each school subject has its own ways of reading, writing, speaking, and thinking that allow individuals to participate in knowledge building (Maton, Hood, & Shay, 2017) and to differentiate "the language of schooling" from everyday uses of language (Bernstein, 1996; Schleppegrell, 2004). Though it is a slow process, the development of students' academic language capacities is really an initiation into new languages—those used within the disciplines.

These new languages require more than the general comprehension and writing strategies used in social contexts or typical literacy courses. Rather, they require a specific set of staged rhetorical structures to satisfy a writing goal in a way that fits the disciplinary context. You have probably already experienced this disciplinary-specific way of engaging in language, though you may not have been explicitly aware of the differences in language between disciplines. For example, suppose you read the following sentence: "This case report describes a 57-year-old man with hemochromatosis and panhypopituitarism who presented with a 6-month history of word-finding difficulty, short-term memory loss, and rapidly cycling symptoms" (Fantaneanu et al., 2016, p. 1150). From this one sentence, you can recognize several things leading you to believe that this text must have come from a medical journal report. We can assume this because the authors use medical terms (hemochromatosis, panhypopituitarism) and medical contexts (patients *presenting* with something and *histories* of symptoms). We might also be able to assume that this is the introduction to a report, considering the syntactical clues in the first sentence ("This case report . . ."), which are being used to orient the reader to the text that follows. Though you read this sentence in a completely isolated state, you were able to use the conventions with which it was written to determine what disciplinary discourse it belongs to. Those specific ways of reading, writing, speaking, and thinking within a specific discipline are known as *disciplinary discourses*. These are the discourses you will be engaging your students in.

Language Demands

In addition to teaching your students the content in your particular subject area, you will also be teaching them the language that is used to communicate that content within your discipline. There are many aspects to language development, but the edTPA focuses on four specific language components: language function, discourse, vocabulary, and syntax (the last three here are collectively referred to as "language demands"). Many teacher candidates become overwhelmed when they reach this point in their portfolio development, but there is no need to panic. Because language is the vehicle through which you teach your content, you are probably already addressing these language demands. You are most likely unfamiliar with the terminology involved and the purposeful planning you can use to support your students as they further develop this language.

What Is a Language Function?

Important to the ways the edTPA expects you to frame and teach your learning segment is the idea that disciplinary texts *purposefully use language*. From word choice to the syntactical structure of written and spoken words, the ways in which each discipline deploys language is meant to do something specific. These specific purposes are called *language functions*, the discourse-specific language that will be used throughout the learning segment. Just as standards and mastery objectives help you align your instruction to a purpose, language functions help you align your language use (and your students' language use) to a specific purpose. Language function refers to what the language *does*—how it functions—throughout your learning segment. In fact, the active verb already stated in the objective (learning goal) of the learning segment often indicates what the language function is.

There should be one clear word or phrase that is the root of the learning you plan for the learning segment. These words and phrases are discipline specific; thus, language functions can vary from one subject matter to another. Figure 5.1 shows examples of appropriate language functions that could direct language decisions throughout a learning segment. Each of these language functions will require appropriately planned supports.

For example, if your goal for the learning segment is for students to *explain* a process, then the language that you should intentionally teach your students to access will be related to the language function *explain*. Similarly, you will be providing supports that enable your students to write explanations, and your summative assessment should challenge students to explain the process stated in your original objective.

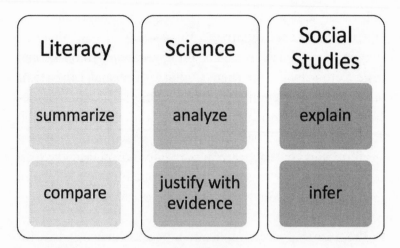

Figure 5.1. Sample language functions by discipline

Beginning with the end in mind... again. Identifying your learning segment's language function is really connected to the process of beginning with the end in mind (Wiggins & McTighe, 2005). Your learning segment's language function is a component of the local, summative assessment that you will use at the end of your learning segment to assess student learning. And just as standards connect learning-segment lessons, so too do language functions. This connectedness between language function and lessons has two important implications:

1 The language function of the learning segment should be evident throughout the learning segment, presented through your instruction and planned learning activities (including formative assessments) and in your students' language use. For example, if you are going to ask the students to explain a phenomenon, you should use terms, structures, and vocabulary related to the process of explaining in addition to the content related to the phenomenon.

2 Because students are to engage in these language functions, a developmental approach to teaching these functions is important. For example, some secondary-level special educators may have their students draw and label event sequences to demonstrate their abilities to explain something. Meanwhile, some secondary-level general education teachers might have their students describe the relevant events and consequences in paragraphs. Both achieve similar purposes of engaging the language function (explain), but they are tailored to the students' learning needs.

These are important implications because they help to drive instructional interactions in the classroom. Far beyond "proper spelling and grammar" judgments, such instruction enables students to access ways of knowing and communicating that are relevant to expert communication. Spelling and grammar are important! More important, however, is the intentional use of language to achieve a purpose. The edTPA requires you to speak about the language function of your learning segment. That purpose is an integral part in your planning, instruction, and assessment. Being clear about your language purpose (the function of the language that you and your students are using across those three to five lessons) is critical to focusing on what is necessary for students to demonstrate in that summative assessment.

How to use language function in the edTPA. In chapter 2, we discussed how lessons build together to form learning segments, which in turn form units, and so on. As these curricular components build, so too do the discourse and language functions integrated into that instruction. Such language building occurs whether it is done intentionally or not. The edTPA asks you to shine a light on the language you are teaching students by demonstrating how you are intentionally building students' disciplinary language.

Your intentional language function instruction is most easily seen in the mastery objectives that you construct for each lesson. To this end, each lesson is its own discourse and has its own language function. For example, if I am teaching a lesson in which I would like my students to summarize act 3, scene 1, of *Romeo and Juliet*, I would construct an exit ticket in which they would summarize that scene. My mastery objectives might read,

Students will be able to

- Identify the main characters in act 3, scene 1, of *Romeo and Juliet*
- Plot five critical moments in the scene in chronological order, focusing on the Prince and what he knows
- Summarize the scene as it pertains to the Prince, (1) providing a background of the scene, (2) providing a chronology of events in the scene, and (3) inferring the importance of these events

Not only is it clear in my last objective that the language function of this lesson is *summary*, but my mastery objectives scaffold students' summarizing discourse by (1) requiring them to recognize and analyze critical summary components (e.g., characters and important events/moments) and (2) detailing how a strong summary is structured. These scaffolds all but ensure that my students will use the language of summary throughout the lesson, particularly focusing on characters, events, chronology, and meaning.

While lessons should have their own language function features, so too should the whole of your learning segment. The summative assessment at the end of your learning segment indicates that there is something to accomplish—something that makes the three to five lessons a coherent whole. As a coherent whole, there is a discourse and language function that cut across the whole learning segment. It is the language function and discourse planned at this level that you will report on during your edTPA commentary.

Let's extend the preceding example by mapping out a potential three-lesson learning segment about *Romeo and Juliet*, focusing specifically on the role of and decisions made by the Prince. Lesson 1 (the lesson described earlier) summarizes the scene in which Romeo has killed Juliet's cousin Tybalt and the Prince banishes Romeo from Verona rather than executing him. A next lesson could be another summary lesson, this time of act 5, scene 3, in which the Friar explains all that happened in the deaths of both Romeo and Juliet at the end of the play. A third lesson might be a compare-and-contrast lesson of the Prince's reactions to these events and what they say about the role of government and leadership in the play.

Notice in this example how Lessons 1 and 2 both employ the language function of *summary*. Yet the third lesson employs the language function of *comparison*. Which is the language function of the whole learning segment?

PLANNING PATHWAYS

Look at your planned learning segment. Based on the central focus and academic standard(s) driving your segment, identify the language function of your segment. In what ways will your students be expected to use this function? In what ways will you support them?

In this case, the two summary lessons are in service to the comparison. The students needed to be able to summarize each scene before they could use that information to compare and contrast the Prince's reactions. More specifically, the summary work allowed the students to (1) chronologically record the events in each scene and (2) consider the importance of these events in light of the Prince, an often-overlooked character. The summary work, rather than just a record of events, lays a framework by which the students can thoughtfully compare and contrast the character of the Prince in Lesson 3. As a whole, then, the learning segment is intentionally designed to support students' comparison, which is the language function of the learning segment. Through lesson plans, instructional explanations, student discussions, and instructional materials, the learning segment's prevailing discourse would also be *comparison*. The discourse and language function features of a learning segment are directly related to the summative assessment of the learning segment and the mastery objectives of each lesson.

Academic Vocabulary

Vocabulary is probably the one aspect of language demands that you are most comfortable with. Literacy courses throughout the country rely on staples of vocabulary research to help teacher candidates understand the intricacies of words and meanings. The research on tiers of vocabulary instruction (e.g., Beck, McKeown, & Kucan, 2013) is extensive and important to our work as teachers. Creating vocabulary-rich environments enables students to engage texts with various contents, syntactic structures, and language functions with greater ease (Shanahan & Shanahan, 2008). Students' abilities to comprehend the meanings of the words on the page are necessary (though not sufficient) for comprehending text (Gallagher, 2009).

Vocabulary, in the context of lesson planning and preparing for the edTPA, however, may be different from the vocabulary you are used to using and planning for. It may indeed be the new terms that are associated with the learning segment you are about to teach, and you will need to continue to provide supports to students for these new terms. But there are also other forms of vocabulary that you will need to consider. One of these additional forms refers to words that the students already know in social language that have different meanings within the discipline. For example, scientists use the word *theory* in a very different way than the general public uses the word. Another common (and adorable) example from elementary school occurs when teachers ask their students what the "difference" is in a math problem. Inevitably, some children start describing qualitative differences between two groups rather than finding the mathematical difference. The edTPA also considers another form of vocabulary, which includes the symbols used in some disciplines such as math and science. These symbols (like pi) may be completely new to students, while others (letters of the alphabet used as specific variables or unit labels) may be familiar to students but used in new ways. Finally, the academic terms that are not specific to your discipline but *are* specific to an academic arena may also be used as vocabulary for a learning segment. For example, a father preparing dinner for his kids doesn't generally ask his kids to "contrast" any two items; it isn't a word that comes up often in social settings. The word *contrast*, however, does not belong to any specific discipline (unless you are talking about artistic disciplines). As a general academic word, it should still be treated as vocabulary. Similarly, words such as *differentiate*, *analyze*, and *synthesize* will require you to support students, especially in lower grade levels, where they have not had much experience with academic language.

Syntax

The edTPA borrows Jeff Zwiers's (2008) idea of *syntax* as "the set of conventions for organizing symbols, words, and phrases together into structures" (Stanford Center for Assessment, Learning, and Equity [SCALE], 2016, p. 47). This is a stronger, more inclusive definition than the one most people know— the way that words are ordered in a sentence. What is valuable about Zwiers's idea of syntax is that there are conventions tying syntax to disciplinary discourse. Thus, there are appropriate (and inappropriate) ways to order words in a sentence, to form sentences, and to order sentences into paragraphs *per discipline*. It also allows for the ordering of symbols, such as those used in equations and formulas, in addition to the syntax of written words.

A simple example of these differences can be made between scientific texts and those in the humanities. Scientific texts are structured on declarative claims, which are always cited. These declarative claims are structured in the third person, focusing on other research and researchers as well as the role of objects of study (e.g., chemicals, animals, stars) to be agents in change-making processes. As such, scientific writing is highly impersonal; even when scientists have to refer to themselves (which is rare), they write in the third person—"the researchers climbed the high cliff" rather than "we."

Contrary to some popular beliefs, few disciplines in the humanities encourage the use of *I*. Writing in the humanities is slightly more personal, though, because of the syntactical structures. The interpretive nature of discourse analysis, for example, requires English professors to use modals (words like *may* and *might*) that declare some level of interpretive uncertainty. The resulting explanations focusing on text analysis require fewer citations per line of written text. While such works are very well researched, the syntactic structure allows for more description and fewer claims per paragraph.

These distinctions are important to your edTPA work because the ways that authors structure their sentences may be different from what you ask your students to do. Whereas you might want your students to read a scholarly review of a particular literary work, for example, your students' writing might not approximate what they are reading. You might allow your students to use *I* because that is where they are in their developmental writing. That is okay! What the edTPA is asking you to do is to recognize such differences in sentence structure and alert students to it either by helping them to understand it or by helping them to emulate it, or both.

Sometimes such explanations can make a big impact on students' comprehension. Historians, for example, sometimes position two sentences next to each other in a paragraph to imply a cause-effect relationship between two things such as a historical figure's feelings and how he reacts: "George Washington withdrew his troops. He feared that he would be overpowered by enemy forces." Notice that there is no conjunction such as *because* or *so* that connects these two sentences. Skilled readers are able to recognize the implied causal relationship, but poor readers don't recognize the relationship, which inhibits their comprehension of the passage (Fitzgerald, 2012). Simply helping students to recognize such patterns can help them to comprehend text better and employ such structures in their own work (Humphrey, 2017).

How vocabulary impacts syntax. In addition to word frequency, pay particular attention to the ways in which vocabulary impacts syntax. One common way in which this occurs is through *nominalization,* when nouns are created from adjectives or verbs (Halliday & Matthiessen, 2004). Nominalization creates a "power grammar" with which writers can pack sentences dense with meaning (Martin, 1989; Rose & Martin, 2012).

For example, a text might read, "The decision to air the video helped the prosecution to win the case." "The decision" is a nominalized form of the verb *to decide.* Nominalizing the verb allows the author to do at least two things:

1 It allows the author to change the subject of the sentence and thus the resulting paragraph. If the author had originally written, "The judge was on the fence about whether to show the video of the murder to the jury," the next sentence would either pick up with the subject of *the judge* or the object *the video.* Picking up the subject or object would allow for the author to construct a coherent text—one in which the sentences fit together. What the author really wants to do, however, is link showing the video to a prosecutorial win. Nominalizing "the decision" ("on the fence" means that "deciding" is taking place) allows the author to pick up on that thread as subject and quickly get to "the win." *Nominalization allows writers to reorder sentences to create a more coherent text.*

2 Nominalizing also allows authors to hide agency. In the preceding example, we aren't quite sure who is doing the deciding. Is it the judge? Is it the prosecution? Is it the deep state?! The authors can circumvent such "in the weeds" questions and conclude the trial's outcome quickly. Nominalization allows readers to ask questions of the text about processes that are obscured by the language, adding a critical lens to reading.

Of course, using nominalized forms of adjectives and verbs rarely has anything to do with deep-state conspiracy theories. Often, they are used for the convenient purposes of sentence order. In other cases, they are used to condense a process that the author assumes the reader already understands. In all cases, nominalizations make the text more formal (Bernstein, 1996). Avid readers of science texts hold a common conception of eroding; they don't need the verb to be in that form for every sentence. In that case, discussing *erosion* makes more sense so that other, new information can be offered.

Combined with upper-tiered words, nominalization helps authors and readers to communicate in more sophisticated ways. The words we use (vocabulary) and the ways in which we structure those words into complex thoughts (syntax) will allow students to code switch more effectively and be able to access a wider variety of texts in the future. Practicing language use really does increase students' abilities to access and build knowledge (Maton et al., 2017).

Syntax and vocabulary in Task 2. The practicing of language skills is what is expected in the edTPA. Task 2 in particular asks you to provide a video demonstration and then discuss the ways that you *and your students* use academic language. Within your learning-segment plans, you should certainly identify potentially problematic or important vocabulary, syntactic, and discourse components. Just as importantly, though, you and your students should verbalize these components, exploring and using them in authentic ways. Beyond "reviewing key vocabulary," your video should show you and your students using and interrogating key vocabulary, thinking about why authors chose to say X instead of Y and questioning the purpose of discourse when necessary (we'll talk more about discourse in the next section). All of these things might not happen in all of your lessons; all of these things probably will not happen in any single lesson either. Throughout your learning segment, you should build in texts (or problems, if you are in math or science) with enough interest and complexity that such inquiry is called from the text and called for within your disciplinary work with your students (Gallagher, 2009). Making that learning explicit is important for the edTPA, but it is more important for your emerging scholars—your students.

Discourse

Academic vocabulary and syntax are the building blocks of discourse. Discourse refers not only to what is said but also to how it is said and the form that the communication takes. In our cases, most school-level academic discourse is in the form of written essays or formal presentations. "What is said" is often related to the academic vocabulary that students use in their writing and speaking. What many teacher candidates still need to consider is "how it is said"—the staged structures of discourses that alert the reader or listener to how communication is structured and builds on itself.

Let's start with an elementary example before we explore various discourse structures. Pretend that you are in first grade again, playing with your friends on the playground. As you climb up the steps to get to the top of the jungle gym, you accidentally push into your friend; she falls and is hurt. When your teacher comes over to you, you say, "I didn't mean to push her. I was climbing up on the steps, and my shoulder accidentally hit her leg, and she tumbled to the ground." In this example, you are clearly providing an explanation for your teacher. You start with the outcome of the situation, "pushing her." Then you proceed to tell the important events that led up to the event. This is an example of explanatory discourse structure—explain the outcome and provide reasons for that outcome.

Imagine again that you are playing with these same friends but instead *you* are the one who is accidently pushed and have tumbled to the ground. When the teacher comes over to you to find out what happened, you might explain, "I was climbing up the steps, and my friend behind me hit into my leg, and I lost balance, and then I tumbled to the ground." Notice that this is also an explanation, but it has a different structure. Instead of starting with the outcome, you start with the relevant details leading up to the event. Here, you end with the outcome. This demonstrates that there are two ways to build an explanation. This type of explanation is called a *consequential explanation*; the previous example is called a *factorial explanation* (Coffin, 2006).

Types of discourse. The preceding examples illustrate that we learn at least some of these discourse structures at a young age. The fictional children in these examples certainly couldn't tell you what a factorial explanation is, but they could construct one nonetheless. As students develop their academic communication skills, they learn various disciplinary ways of structuring communication—like descriptions, explanations, comparisons, and arguments. These discourses have specific stages that readers and writers commonly understand, aiding text comprehension and communication.

Table 5.1, based on Caroline Coffin's (2006) work, outlines these basic discourse structures. You might notice that these structures sound similar to the language functions discussed at the beginning of this chapter. That is because the two are

Table 5.1. Example Discourse Structures (adapted from Coffin, 2006)

Description	Explanation	Comparison	Argument
Recount • Background • Record of events (what)	**Factorial** • Outcome • Factors	**Compare and contrast** • One way • Another way • Similarities • Differences	**Discussion** • Background • Thesis • Arguments • Position
Account • Background • Account of events (why)	**Consequential** • Input • Consequences		**Challenge** • Background • Position challenged • Arguments • Antithesis

related. The discourse structures help the language fulfill its purpose. For example, providing a description of one text, a description of another, similarities between the two, and differences between the two helps the language fulfill the function of *comparison*. If any of those pieces were missing, the comparison would be incomplete.

Relationship between discourse and syntax. Certain discourse structures use certain organizational markers to achieve the language function. These markers are often related to syntax. Returning to the playground example, you notice that the fictional children use *and* as a conjunctive marker. (Breathless first graders also speak in run-on sentences!) This use of *and* could also be replaced with *then*. Both conjunctive markers order the stories chronologically. Descriptions and explanations often use chronological language to order the discourse.

Comparison and argumentative discourse structures may use some chronology, but such chronology is usually found in the explanations embedded in the large structure. For example, if I were arguing that the Storm Troopers were actually the good guys in the *Star Wars* movies, I would have to provide examples.* Those examples might entail some chronological explanations of scenes that support my argument. Across these discourse structures, however, I would also expect to use cause-effect language because I am not only making my argument but countering other arguments as well. These elements of chronological and argumentative language relate to syntax in the way we order the language inside the discourse.

Relationship between discourse and the summative assessment. Because there is such a close relationship between your learning segment's language function and discourse structure, it is useful to use the discourse structure that most closely relates to your language function as the basis for the Task 3 summative assessment. The edTPA requires candidates to explain how the language function is used throughout the learning segment. If, for example, I wanted students to compare and contrast two Civil War soldiers' points of view on the Emancipation Proclamation (using *comparison* as my language function), it would make sense that my summative assessment would be a compare-and-contrast essay. Using the structure of that discourse, I can create my rubric, knowing that I will want students to explain both points of view, describe similarities between those views, and describe differences. We'll talk more about Task 3 in chapter 7. For now, know that the language elements of your learning segment relate not just to your instruction but to your assessment as well.

---

* Neither of us actually believes this argument. Please don't send us hate mail! :)

Language Supports

Planning for instruction includes purposeful planning to incorporate academic language. Teacher candidates may not be as familiar with this component of planning as they are with other instructional language practices, namely, those learned in literacy courses. In the United States, there is a large and important focus on literacy—strategies to support students' fluency and comprehension of texts. Such instruction is critical to supporting various students in their literacy journeys. What literacy instruction is not so good at is demonstrating the language resources that authors use to compose various types of texts, particularly those types of texts most valued by different disciplines. For such a demonstration, an exploration into the ways that authors make meaning across various types of texts has proven helpful for teaching students how systems of language work for particular purposes.

Meaningful, Whole-Class Supports

Because academic language and social language diverge so greatly, most of your students will only ever experience and practice academic language in the classroom. They do not get to experience it at home or with their friends, and so it is important for you to build in supports for every language demand you place on your students. The supports you provide will allow for differentiation, scaffolding, and a more equitable learning environment for your diverse students.

As an emerging teacher, you will want to begin with planning for whole-class supports. These supports are the tried-and-true strategies that many teachers employ in a wide variety of settings to help all of the students in the class access the new language. They are generally implemented by you and

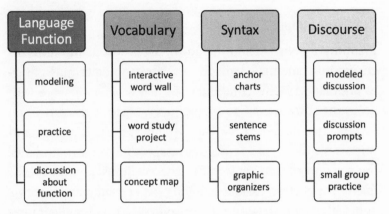

Figure 5.2. Sample whole-class supports

will serve as a base on which your targeted supports can grow. Though instructional strategies change over time and by subject area, figure 5.2 provides some suggestions for whole-class supports according to the language demand they most closely support. Of course, there is some overlap among language demands, so some of these suggestions may also carry over into other language-demand categories as well.

Targeted Supports

As we have discussed the need to vary your instructional approaches and activities to meet the needs of your diverse learners, you are again challenged to employ varied language instruction to meet the needs of your students. In developing targeted supports, you should be mindful of the fact that the student groupings you planned for as you varied content instruction may differ from what you plan to do here. Students who struggle or excel in the content area may not be the same students who struggle or excel in acquiring academic language (though they may be). The targeted supports you plan here should be for the students who need specific help in using one or more of your planned language demands. These supports can be implemented individually or with small groups of students sharing a similar need.

The good news is that you generally won't have to develop these supports from scratch; instead you can tier the supports you already planned for the whole class. For example, let's assume you have three Spanish-speaking students in your mainstream class of twenty-four. You are teaching students about the layers of the atmosphere using an interactive notebook as your whole-class vocabulary support. The class will be writing out the new words on the foldable layers of the notebook demonstrating the levels of the atmosphere. To tier this activity, you can help your ESL students to record the English words on one side with the Spanish translations on the other. This type of support shows that you understand the needs not only of your whole class but of the individual students who make up your class as well.

Another example of tiering your supports may be to first provide a sentence stem or sentence frame for your students as a whole-class syntax support. It will help to ensure that your students understand how to properly phrase a relationship. "As mass _____, gravity _____." There are quite a lot of things you could do with this simple sentence. It is familiarizing your students with the syntax used within the discipline of science. Of course, they could just as easily say, "When something gets bigger, its gravity is stronger." The two sentences mean the same thing, but the frame you have given the students is helping them to structure their language in a way that is aligned with the discipline (the way a scientist would say it). Notice the blanks leave the statement somewhat open-ended.

Students will have a choice in what word they insert into the first blank (*increases* or *decreases*), but they will have to make sure that the way they complete the second blank accurately completes the sentence (either both blanks will say *increases*, or both will say *decreases*). Now to tier this simple support, you should consider your more academically gifted students and your struggling students. The specific frame you give your students could be varied based on their ability level. For your more highly achieving students, consider simply giving them a sentence starter rather than a whole frame or withdrawing this support completely later in the year as their skills develop further. Starting their sentence with "As mass increases, _____" will challenge them to model the second part of the sentence after the first part. They will recognize the importance in mirroring the phrases and will therefore not respond with a statement about gravity "getting stronger." For your struggling students, you can return to the original sentence frame but possibly remove one of the blanks so that there is a correct answer rather than a choice. Under the blank that remains, list multiple choice options (*increases, decreases, stays the same*) to eliminate the risk of the students slipping into social language stating that it will "get bigger." Manipulating a support this way provides students with the targeted help they most need.

After reviewing these suggestions and examples, it is our hope that you recognize the importance but also the feasibility of supporting your students in their language development. Because it is an area of instruction that greatly allows for differentiation, you are making the learning more equitable across the students in your classroom; you are providing access to a more sophisticated level of communication to all of your students regardless of their prior experiences and socioeconomic status.

You have already planned for the language function of your learning segment earlier in this chapter. Take a few minutes now to identify the other
language demands you will be using in your learning segment. What types
of whole-class and targeted supports will you be able to offer your students?

Understanding Students' Use of Academic Language

The final piece of academic language you will need to address
in your edTPA is your assessment of academic language use.
*SCALE: Rubric 14 challenges you to discuss the academic language
used by your students.* It is not enough for you to plan supports
to introduce this new language to your students. You must also
recognize when they use it and how well they use it. The good
news is that the edTPA is not providing you a score based on
how well your students use academic language (phew!). What
they are looking for is that you can accurately describe your
students' language use. If the students are still struggling,
that is okay. You have to describe it as such. If your students
are excelling, good for you! Write it up. What will cause you
problems here is if your students are clearly not doing well
(as evinced by their work samples and video footage) but you
try to say they are doing well. Similarly, if your students are
using academic language in appropriate ways (again in their
work and in the video) but you do not reference it, the scorers
will question how well you understand the language of your
own discipline. Be honest and descriptive. You may use specific examples from your students' work or comment on video
footage by suggesting a time stamp for the scorer to review
that will bring attention to the fact that you are aware of the
language developing all around you.

Placing Academic Language into a Broader Context

The ways in which people engage in the disciplines directly impact the ways in which they conceptualize the information they learn. Our "knowing" is conveyed through language. Each discipline has its own ways of thinking and communicating. Thus, each school subject "can be regarded as a disciplinary discourse . . .with specific ways of reading, writing, speaking, doing, and thinking, which differs from daily perspectives on the world" (Larsson, 2018, p. 61). Helping students to engage in these disciplinary discourses requires them to implement the other language demands—the function of the language, the meaning and uses of terms, the ways in which ideas can be ordered, and the ways that texts can be structured. It also requires students to learn to think in disciplinary ways, engaging in similar disciplinary problem-solving processes as disciplinary experts. Together, we can call these two learning requirements *disciplinary ways of thinking.*

Disciplinary Ways of Thinking. In addition to constructivism, the edTPA preferences disciplinary ways of thinking. ***SCALE: The preference of the edTPA toward disciplinary ways of thinking is present in the rubrics' focus on disciplinary language (see your handbook's definitions of* academic language, vocabulary, *and* discourse*) and disciplinary reasoning (see the specific disciplinary skills you need to attend to in the criteria for Rubric 1, Level 4, and Rubric 9).*** To the extent that our language is functionally appropriate to a particular language community (Halliday & Matthiessen, 2004), a focus on disciplinary language necessitates students' knowledge of and comfort with using appropriate disciplinary ways of speaking and writing about disciplinary texts and experiences (e.g., science labs). It is through the teacher's support and the students' development and use of disciplinary language and skills that students can construct and communicate in disciplinary discourses.

Implications for Instructional Materials. This preference for disciplinary ways of thinking and communicating suggests that the more a teacher candidate includes authentic texts and experiences beyond "the textbook," the better students will be able to express their own disciplinary understanding in authentic ways.

This is not to suggest that students can't use disciplinary language when they work with less authentic texts and experiences; their ability to do so does diminish, though. For example, when Sam Wineburg (2001) asked students of varying abilities to discuss the reliability of sources, they routinely selected textbook passages above eyewitness accounts, a particularly false assumption given the texts he selected for his study. It was not that these students didn't know what reliability was but that they had not had the experience to appropriately engage in such historical thinking. To the extent that we are able to engage students with disciplinary texts and experiences, students will be more comfortable and capable employers of disciplinary language.

Summary

The ways in which we use language in any discipline are encoded in the ways that we think in that discipline (Schleppegrell, 2004; Zwiers, 2014). Whether you are engaging students in comprehension or composition throughout your learning segment, you are engaging them in the thinking and language skills important to the discipline. This engagement should go beyond the vocabulary that your students may find difficult and toward apprenticeship into the language of the discipline.

A word of caution, though—depending on (1) the academic language abilities of your students and (2) their language abilities related to the topic you are teaching (and these are two different things), you need to be explicit about what is important in any given text *and* sensitive to the learning curve of academic language. You, as expert, are so accustomed to academic language within your discipline that, for you, describing and using academic language features is like a fish trying to describe water (Zwiers, 2014). You know how to appropriately comprehend and compose such texts. Your students, on the other hand, do not; this is especially true for students who are not from home cultures where academic language is practiced (Heath, 1983). Be patient, go slow, and teach explicitly the ways that academic language works in incremental pieces. This is one learning segment—don't overdo it! More importantly, your students are human beings—don't squash their desire to learn this "new language" with constant admonitions. We are all—and forever will be—language learners.

ORIENTATION
Where Are You Now?

1 What is academic language, and how is it used in the classroom?

2 How are language demands different from language supports?

3 What is discourse, and why do you believe it is such an important part of your portfolio?

CHAPTER 6

Fostering a Challenging Learning Environment

ORIENTATION

You Are Here

Throughout your own general education and in your teacher preparation program, you have been immersed in different learning environments. You will have seen different styles and techniques teachers use to organize student learning and develop their classroom cultures.

This chapter will serve to highlight important approaches and techniques you can use in your own classroom that are aligned with edTPA expectations and connected to the environment you hope to establish for your students.

Building Rapport with Students

Your class climate and ability to promote a challenging learning environment will depend largely on your relationship with your students. The process of building rapport with students is often overlooked as it is something that can happen, intentionally or unintentionally, over time. The relationship you have with your students, however, will directly impact the quality of learning that takes place in your classroom. It is therefore imperative that you purposely create the type of relationships that will build rapport with your students.

The best approach to appropriate teacher-student relationships is to consider the old story of Goldilocks and the Three Bears. As Goldilocks learns when she samples the bears' porridge, one is too hot, one is too cool, and the last is "just right." With students, you will see that some teachers favor one extreme or the other. For example, you will see some teachers in your building who may yell at children and strip them of privileges on a regular basis, even for minor transgressions. These teachers make no exceptions for late homework, even when the student has a valid excuse. These teachers often complain about their students in the teachers' lounge and seem directly and personally offended when students don't do well in their classes. They may believe that showing empathy toward their students will allow their students to take advantage in class. Let's say that these teachers' methods are "too hot" in our Goldilocks analogy and may result in students disliking school.

In your student teaching placement or from your personal experiences, you may also have witnessed teachers who approach student relationships from the opposite extreme. It often seems these teachers do not know how to say no to students. They will accept late work without penalty. When students ask for extra credit, extra time, or a later date to take a test, these teachers willingly oblige. Being overly forgiving in these situations will not set up a positive classroom environment, even though these teachers hope it will. In reality, these methods create issues in the class. Students who perform their work well and on time will often feel the teacher is unfair to let so many students slide. If your students believe you are showing favoritism or that you do not follow through on expectations, they will become less motivated to learn.

More alarmingly, some teachers even try to befriend their students. Teachers in this group enjoy allowing the students to get off topic for the sake of socialization. They participate in students' conversations in inappropriate ways. You will, of course, converse with your students, but it should be in a mentorship role and preferably when invited to do so rather than as an intrusion into students' social circles. It is important to remember that you serve a different role as an educator; you are not your students' friend. Dressing and speaking professionally will help to serve as a reminder to your students, and to yourself, that your purpose in the classroom is to educate children in a developmentally and culturally responsive way. Do not make the mistake of being the "too cool" porridge.

Building rapport with students should be "just right" and happen naturally. Rapport is more than simply being nice to students, and it is even more than showing respect within a classroom; Brandi Frisby and Matthew Martin (2010) define rapport as "an overall feeling between two people encompassing a mutual, trusting, and prosocial bond" (p. 147). The respect and care you show toward your students should be mutual and for the benefit of all of the individuals within your class. *SCALE: The edTPA will be looking at the ways you interact with students. A simple "good job" or thumbs-up shown to a student is not enough evidence that you have built rapport; the entire class climate showing mutual respect among you and your students will provide more evidence that this pattern of respect is consistent for your classroom. When a positive climate is developed within your class, your students will feel more comfortable and supported to take risks and make connections as they learn.*

Fostering a Challenging Environment

The idea of fostering a challenging learning environment really has two essential components: providing opportunities for complex thinking and the physical use of classroom space. Providing opportunities for complex thinking includes questioning techniques to incite higher-order thinking and the ability to facilitate prosocial student interactions. Challenging students to think deeply (also referred to as providing a *rigorous* learning experience) has shown to increase both student achievement (Hattie, 2011) and student engagement (Newmann, 1992), which is why it is such an important part of preparing your teacher performance portfolio. *SCALE: Within the edTPA, Rubric 6 directly addresses the learning environment you create for your students and the rapport you show with them. Rubric 8 will assess how well you elicit and build on students' responses to develop higher-order thinking within your classroom.*

Questioning Techniques and Higher-Order Thinking

Benjamin Bloom's (1956) taxonomy organizes cognitive demands into a pyramid with the least cognitively demanding thinking at the bottom (recall and understand) and the most demanding at the top (evaluate and create). As you develop your lesson objectives, you will be using verbs to represent the tasks you are asking students to do. These verbs will relate to specific levels of the taxonomy and should therefore be chosen with care. Spending a few minutes to carefully craft your objectives based on the standards (while providing the necessary support for your students to accomplish them) will maximize the learning potential of your students.

You can also use the verbs strategically while questioning students to ensure that higher-order thinking is taking place

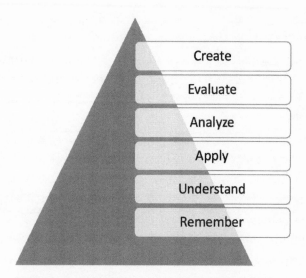

Figure 6.1. Bloom's revised taxonomy (Krathwohl, 2002)

during class activities and discussions. You will not immediately jump into evaluation and synthesis questions, as your students may not be ready to answer. Instead, you can walk your students up the pyramid, so to speak. Build up to higher-order thinking by laying the groundwork with lower-order questions. You may begin a discussion with factual knowledge. Many teachers, and especially pre-service teachers, are delighted when a student answers correctly. They praise the student for answering correctly and then quickly move on to another fact-based question. Instead, you can (and should) continue to discuss the same concept by layering your questions. Figure 6.2 depicts an example of a class discussion that uses this layering technique.

An added benefit to this questioning strategy is that it provides an easy way to differentiate for your students. Starting with lower-order questions provides struggling students a chance to participate in whole-class instruction with success.

Teacher: What are earthquakes? (Teacher waits for several hands to be raised before calling on a student.) Hailey.

Hailey: They're vibrations, like the Earth is shaking.

Teacher: They are the vibrations, yes, that carry... what?

Hailey: Energy?

Teacher: Perfect! They carry energy! Can anyone tell me why we have earthquakes? Yes, Melissa.

Melissa: Because there are faults?

Teacher: Yes, thank you. There are faults in many places along Earth's surface. Where can you find these faults?

Luis: California!

Teacher: California! That's certainly true. We hear of many earthquakes happening in California, don't we? We don't, however, hear of many earthquakes in some other states like... North Dakota, for example. Did anyone ever watch a news report about all of the earthquakes in North Dakota? (A few students shake their heads to indicate they had not.) So, what is so different between California and North Dakota? Why would there be so many earthquakes in California and almost none in North Dakota? (Teacher turns to erase chalkboard, building in wait time for students to think.)

Teacher: Ajay, I can see you thinking. What have you come up with? Why might California have so many more earthquakes than North Dakota?

Ajay: Well, because, it's right by the ocean, it's on a coastline but North Dakota isn't.

Teacher: Great! Can anyone add to Ajay's answer? Why is California's location so important?

Sanjana: It's on a plate boundary. Like when we learned about the volcanoes, the earthquakes are happening there too because it's a plate boundary.

Teacher: I love the connection you made to our volcano unit! Now before you respond to my next question, I am going to ask for you to Think-Pair-Share for this one. Why would earthquakes occur in the same places that many volcanoes exist? Think for a moment on your own, then turn to your partner and discuss your ideas. We will share as a class in a few minutes.

Figure 6.2. Hypothetical classroom discussion using multiple levels of questioning

Provide the proper amount of wait time and then select a student who traditionally has difficulty in the subject area. There are always eager students with their hands up for every question; they can wait and be called on at appropriate intervals. In this way, all of the students in your class will have an equal chance to participate, and you have leveled the playing field; the questions you have posed to all of your students will challenge them at their own particular learning levels.

In your teacher preparation program, you may have used a Q Chart or Questioning Grid to plan out higher-order-thinking questions. This grid, shown in figure 6.3, can be used to craft questions aligned to specific orders of thinking. When you pair the word in front of each row and at the top of each column, the question you generate will fall into a specific quadrant in the grid. The quadrant tells you what level of question you are asking and to what order of thinking your student will rise in order to provide an answer. This questioning grid is likely to become cumbersome if you try to use it too often while you are implementing your lessons. Instead, we recommend you use it as a tool as you plan your lessons. Come up with three to five strong higher-order-thinking questions ahead of time that you can include directly in your plan. As you gain experience in using this technique in the classroom, the development of these questions will become habitual to the point that you no longer need to rely on the physical chart.

Analyzing the classroom discussion in figure 6.2 will reveal that the teacher began with a lower-order, "remembering"-level question: "*What are* earthquakes?" She doesn't simply accept the student's answer as right or wrong but continues to help the student build on the response by considering why the ground is actually shaking (energy). The teacher then takes the same concept and increases the level of cognitive complexity by asking, "*Why are* there earthquakes?" Again, she extends

	Is/Are	Can	Did/Do	Would	Will	Might
Who						
What	Remembering and Understanding			Applying		
When						
Where						
Why	Analyzing			Evaluating and Creating		
How						

Figure 6.3. Questioning Grid / Q Chart

the discussion to analyze why they occur in some places more than others. She concludes the discussion with a Think-Pair-Share strategy for the highest order of thinking question. She asks the students, "*Why would* earthquakes occur in the same locations as volcanoes?" Using the Think-Pair-Share strategy provides a level of support for students who struggle with questions of this level of cognitive demand.

PLANNING PATHWAYS

Use the Q Chart shown in figure 6.3 to write a total of eight questions that can be applied to what you or your cooperating teacher are teaching. You should have two questions in each quadrant. Ideally, these questions should relate to the learning segment you are planning to teach for your teacher performance assessment.

Constructivist Approaches and Student-Centered Learning

Throughout this book, we have been pointing out that the edTPA has definite preferences for specific pedagogy and assessment strategies. These preferences are based in research on best practices in education. Constructivism is the underlying psychological theory of learning that is preferred by the edTPA and the common thread connecting many of the other instructional approaches and decisions we have discussed thus far.

Constructivism was born from the cognitive theories of Jean Piaget and Lev Vygotsky and amended by many psychologists and educational researchers for decades (Fosnot, 2005). The term has branched out to encompass multiple forms of constructivist approaches, which may blur the term's clarity. Constructivism draws from three learner roles: the active learner, the social learner, and the creative learner (Perkins, 1999). Literature can take these and other roles and extend them so that they appear to be very different approaches in education. In reality, there is often overlap among these learner roles; students can be actively engaged and working cooperatively with others, while simultaneously creating their understanding of a concept. Each of these roles demands that the learner work toward constructing their own knowledge.

Regardless of which specific approach you are comfortable employing within your classroom, the main goal is that you do rely on some constructivist theory. Within your secondary classroom, you may feel that one of the aforementioned approaches is better suited to your own teaching style or to the learning styles of your students than the other approaches are. You may also blend these approaches or rely on them at different points within your instruction. What will need to be obvious to an outside observer (such as your principal or edTPA scorer) is the way in which you engage students to construct understanding of the content within your learning segment.

What might a constructivist approach look like in your classroom? A signature feature of constructivist learning is its active, student-centered pedagogy. The role of a teacher has expanded over the course of formalized education implementation (November, 2012). Teachers, at one time, were expected to have all the answers and to tell the students everything they need to know. Anyone who has spent time in twenty-first-century classrooms will immediately recognize that this is no longer the case. Teachers today are expected to facilitate learning by activating students' prior knowledge and engaging them in tasks that will challenge assumptions and build new knowledge. *SCALE: Rubric 7 will be looking for evidence that you have done just that.* Additionally, teachers today must employ inquiry-based instructional practices and implement suitable technology to foster students' creative thinking and collaboration skills.

These changes in instructional practices will be evident to a trained observer through several features of your lesson. An observer will most likely see the teacher circulating the room and trouble-shooting with students. The teacher may be using questioning strategies rather than direct lecture to elicit and build on students' responses. Students will most likely be working in groups to solve problems, gather evidence, or debate concepts. These classrooms may have many things going on all at once rather than the single method of delivery used in the past. Similarly, these classrooms will probably be full of more noise and discussion than they had in the past. Novice teachers are sometimes nervous in these instances, thinking that the volume in the classroom is indicative of poor classroom management skills. On the contrary, engaged students, though potentially loud while many groups are involved in simultaneous discussions, indicate a positive classroom climate.

Student-centered becoming student-driven. You may have heard the terms *student-centered* and *student-driven* instruction at some point during your teacher preparation coursework. Though these two terms sound similar and are certainly closely related, they are not the same. As we have discussed in the preceding section, student-centered instruction literally revolves around the students. The students are "at the center" of your instructional design. They will therefore be active participants in the learning process. Student-driven, in contrast, takes the student-centered approach to the next level. For students to truly drive instruction, they will have a greater sense of autonomy in planning instruction themselves. They will have a voice in what content is studied and/or the manner in which the content is studied. Of course, this doesn't mean they have command over instructional decisions; instead, you might offer choices that fall within the parameters of the standard you wish to teach. For example, if you need to teach students about ecological interactions, allow the students to decide what ecosystem(s) to study. You may find that your original plan to teach about tropical rainforest relationships falls by the wayside as your secondary students feel the topic is too elementary for them. They may want to challenge themselves to learn about the alien species that live along hydrothermal vents in the ocean instead. Or the students may break into naturally formed groups choosing different ecosystems to study. With regard to instructional design, your students may decide that they want to engage in a beach cleanup when studying human impact on the environment, or they may prefer to look at satellite images demonstrating deforestation over a specific time period. The point is that student-driven lessons are driven by the interests, and inquiring nature, of the students.

Facilitating Student Interactions

The phrase *facilitating student interactions* probably conjures an image of group work in your mind. Cooperative learning groups are certainly a large part of this process, but true facilitation of student interactions—those that lead to actual learning—is a deeper process than simply letting your students work in groups. Think back to your own time as a student. You will have certainly experienced working with a group of peers throughout your own education. There may have been advantages to this group work, but you can probably also recognize its disadvantages. This section discusses some of those costs and benefits associated with student interactions in addition to approaches that will allow for more authentic interactions among your students.

Grouping strategies. When students work in groups, there is more to consider than simply the physical grouping of student desks. Putting students into groups probably seems like an easy thing to do, but it isn't always. Depending on your goal for student learning, some grouping strategies may be more effective than others. A teacher candidate's favorite grouping method seems to be placing advanced students with struggling students, assuming the advanced students would be able to help their struggling peers. Is this really the most effective grouping you could make as a teacher? We have all witnessed this, and probably have worked in these groups ourselves, and know that very often the advanced student feels they are doing "all the work" and the struggling student is taking the credit or receiving the same grade with less effort. Some advanced students don't want to spend the time to reteach material to their peers and will just share their answers so they can be done with the activity and move on. Of course, there are times when these partnerships work well, but they should be chosen with a specific rationale in mind.

You may consider partnering homogeneously, placing students together with similar abilities. It will help you to differentiate your instruction for your students. You can tailor the assignment to provide greater challenge to an entire group of advanced students and provide additional supports for struggling students. Grouping students with peers on the same level could also create a more comfortable group dynamic in which students are more willing to take risks and to participate who may not have been willing to speak up otherwise. Other grouping options include allowing students to choose their own groups or purposefully assigning students to groups based on social behaviors or interests. Allowing students to choose groups again increases autonomy and prevents students from arguing about an unfair workload; after all, they chose their own partners. You may choose groups for social rather than academic reasons if you have students whom you want to work together for a specific reason. This might be to influence a shy student to open up or to force two students with difficult personalities to have to find ways of working together to complete a goal.

Disadvantages and advantages. When students work together, we know that several problems may arise. Though the students may indeed be active and interacting with one another, these behaviors are often unrelated to academic learning or exhibited in off-task behavior (Leikin & Zaslavsky, 1997). In group work, there may often be one or two students who do all of the "work" while the other students socialize. In contrast, sometimes the more advanced students dominate the less competent students (Fredrick, 2008). Students with less competence can also be too embarrassed to ask their peers for help with concepts they don't understand (Leikin & Zaslavsky, 1997). The hierarchy in typical classrooms places teachers in a position of power over the students and the students in positions that are equal to one another; this hierarchy does not model the type of collaborative work students will engage in once they enter the workforce, which makes classroom group work difficult for students to navigate (Fredrick, 2008).

When teachers skillfully position students to interact with one another, however, there can also be educational gains. Students can become more active in the learning process when collaboration is used effectively (Leikin & Zaslavsky, 1997). They will be practicing negotiation and conflict-resolution skills that will benefit them in future coursework and in their eventual careers (Fredrick, 2008). The key to these advantages lies with the teacher, as the teacher is responsible for effectively designing group projects, understanding the process that students will need to engage in during group work, and intervening appropriately to further promote positive student interactions.

The teacher's role. Terri Fredrick (2008) challenges teachers to critically consider the assignments they pose to groups of students. Consider the following questions:

> Accepting that our education system most often supports individual achievement, teachers should begin by critically questioning whether their assignments really value the *process* of teamwork. As designed, is the project too big for an individual to complete without help? Do students have to work together to define, research, and write the project, or could they easily divide the project into individual parts that are then stitched together at the end? Does the project take into account the different skills and experiences team members bring to the project? Does the project schedule provide students with sufficient in-class and out-of-class meeting time in the earliest stages of a project (during brainstorming and preliminary planning), when students are most likely to negotiate their authority relationships? (Fredrick, 2008, p. 448)

Your answers to these questions will help you determine how successful your students will be in their collaborative efforts. If you believe that your assignment may be easily completed by students dividing work or you believe that the students will not be relying on their collective skills as a group to accomplish a group goal, you should consider redesigning your project expectations. A well-designed project that focuses on the process of group collaboration will lead to more successful student outcomes.

Once your project is designed, you should try to anticipate what your students' discussions may be like. Traditionally, the lack of an established hierarchy or defined roles within the group will lead to two different approaches your students may take. The students may engage in transfer-of-knowledge sequences, which approximate the typical discussions held between students and teachers (Fredrick, 2008). One student assumes the "teacher role," guiding the discussion by asking and answering questions posed to the remaining group members. You may also see true collaborative sequences, which are more symmetrical than transfer-of-knowledge sequences; the students equally participate in the discussion without any individual directing the group (Fredrick, 2008). Even within these sequences, you may notice one student trying to dominate the decision-making power of the group, one student not participating in the discussion, or nonacademic chatter. Carefully monitor the students' interactions in each group. You will quickly be able to decide which groups require your intervention.

There are several potential interventions you could provide to keep your students on track. Consider modeling the type of discussion you expect (by asking and answering questions, turn taking, etc.) to ensure all students are actively participating. Provide students with distinct roles so that they each have a specified type of authority to exercise within the group. Decide how much chatter is acceptable and impose a time limit; often students use the nonacademic discussion to strengthen relationships and reduce the anxiety that group conflict creates. You may also hold discussions about the purposes of teamwork or allow the students to write out their own team goals (Fredrick, 2008). Student self-evaluations can be used for the purposes of students reflecting on their own interaction styles.

Similarly, anonymous peer evaluations, weekly/daily team progress reports submitted by members on a rotating basis, or a running log of team conflicts and resolutions can allow you some insight into the process of collaboration taking place in each group.

Though these interventions can be applied across a range of group projects, you may consider using a more structured approach to student collaboration that can be used within your daily routine. Roza Leikin and Orit Zaslavsky (1997) used an experimental model of group work that improved students' attitudes toward working together while increasing the students' time spent as active rather than passive learners. In this experimental model, students worked in pairs within a larger group of four. Each student was assigned a specific problem to solve. The students would solve their own problems, teach the process to their partners, and assist their partners in solving the problems. The students would then switch partners so that they all had the opportunity to act as "teachers" to one another while working through the other problems at their tables. For you to use a similar model in your own classroom, you would need to plan in advance what questions or problems your students would be working through and provide them with specific cards or worksheets to guide them. This model has been shown to increase students' engagement and to reduce off-task behavior (Leikin & Zaslavsky, 1997).

Finally, the length and frequency with which you intervene can affect students' abilities to learn while in cooperative groups (Ding, Li, Piccolo, & Kulm, 2007). Spending too much time with one group means that you are not going to have enough time to equitably work with your other students. Obviously, spending too little time with them might also mean that you are not providing enough support or are allowing the students to get off task. As you have read throughout this book, this is yet another instructional decision that should be made based on the students within your classroom. Spending time with each group to ensure students are on the right track and offering guidance when they are not is vital, but you should also build in time for the students to think through the interventions you provided before returning to check their progress. If you find that many students have the same problems, you can also consider pulling the whole class back together to reteach the problematic concept before the group work continues (Ding et al., 2007). Regardless of which strategy you employ in your class, it is your job to ensure that your students are making educational gains through the use of the collaborative learning process and to intervene when they are not.

Subject-Specific Pedagogies

As you have learned, each academic subject has its own specific disciplinary way to communicate. Similarly, each academic subject has a set of pedagogical practices that are unique. *SCALE: Rubric 9 intends to measure your performance on the use of subject-specific pedagogy.* When you look directly at your edTPA handbook, Rubric 9 will list the specific pedagogy that scorers are expecting to see evinced in your video. This will vary based on the secondary subject you teach.

English Language Arts (ELA) teachers are expected to utilize textual references in ways that help their students to construct meaning from, interpret, or respond to a complex text. Social studies teachers are expected to facilitate their students' use of evidence from sources to analyze or build arguments. Science teachers should have their students gather, record, and find patterns in data. Math teachers will need to use representations in ways that build students' understanding of mathematical concepts. The K–12 handbooks have specific guidelines for music, art, physical education, and world-language teachers as well. Because each of these pedagogies is specific to a discipline, your work will be evaluated only by other members within your discipline.

These pedagogical expectations should be the basis for the work your students are engaging in during at least one of your two video clips. Be mindful of clearly demonstrating (in the video) and explaining (in the commentary) how you were engaging in these processes with your students. Be aware of rubric progressions here as well. If you can use your specific pedagogy well in learning segments leading up to the one you have planned for your edTPA, you may be able to reach for a Level 5 by deepening your students' experience in it during the edTPA learning segment. As you read your specific Rubric 9, you will notice some major differences in Level 3 and Level 5 expectations. Level 5 requires students to take more ownership of the learning (such as strategically selecting their own texts) or may ask you to facilitate interactions in student groups rather than directly teaching the content or skill to the students.

PLANNING PATHWAYS

Open your edTPA handbook to Rubric 9. What pedagogy are you supposed to demonstrate in your learning segment? What evidence will your scorer *see* in your video? What evidence will your scorer *read* in your commentary? How can you alter your plans to move from a Level 3 to a Level 5 score?

Learning Environment

Teachers are responsible for developing a low-risk yet challenging learning environment for their students, which will ultimately impact students' abilities to engage in learning tasks and develop socially. Without properly developing and maintaining an appropriate learning environment, teachers' best efforts in planning and instruction may never come to fruition; a well-planned lesson will go awry when the classroom is not conducive to student learning. To plan for a challenging, low-risk learning environment, teacher candidates need to consider classroom management techniques and the effective use of physical classroom space.

Classroom Management

Classroom management is a term often used in teacher preparation programs and has been a focus of educational research for more than four decades. Teachers, over time, develop their own classroom management styles by synthesizing their coursework in their teacher preparation programs, professional development experiences, and intuition that has been honed by years of experience. Teacher candidates lack this experience and will therefore often struggle with classroom management strategies. It is important, then, to rely on evidence-based techniques. Brandi Simonsen, Sarah Fairbanks, Amy Briesch, Diane Myers, and George Sugai (2008) review decades of research in this area and identify evidence-based best practices along five common themes that will be discussed in this chapter. Teacher candidates can activate these strategies within their own classes by carefully designing systems before teaching, establishing structure and high expectations, and being responsive during the lesson.

Before teaching. Putting some strategies into place at the beginning of the school year can serve as a framework on which the students in your classroom rely to develop appropriate

Suggested Classroom Activities
to Build Positive Relationships

- Try fun games that allow everyone in the class (including you) to learn and remember each others' names
- Create classroom rules with the help of your students, and post them in the classroom
- Hold a brief Morning Meeting each day (or Monday Meeting each week for secondary grades) to welcome your students and allow them to share stories with the class or ask and answer questions unrelated to the curriculum
- Praise student effort and participation rather than accuracy in responses

Figure 6.4. Building positive relationships (Charney, 2002)

relationships throughout the remainder of the year. Ruth Charney (2002) explains that we cannot expect children in our classrooms to do the right thing unless we purposely teach them what "right" is. We do this by setting clear expectations, modeling those expectations, and following through in our daily routines.

One of the first things that happens in classrooms at the beginning of the school year is some sort of discussion of classroom rules. Rules are a necessary part of the learning community at every grade level (Charney, 2002). It is easier for children to stay within boundaries when they have a clear understanding of what those boundaries are and what would happen as a result if any line is crossed throughout the year. Many veteran teachers advocate for class-generated rules;

students are more willing to follow the rules they help create because they assisted in the process and have an authentic understanding of the need for the rules. Right away at the beginning of the year, you can discuss with your students what rules and consequences they would like to see in place in their classroom (yes, theirs—not yours).

Brainstorm a list of suggestions with your students and write them up on the board or on large paper so everyone can see. Using too many rules and too many words within the rules is never a good strategy. Work with your students to combine some of the expectations into a list of about five clear guidelines that can be applied across different scenarios. For example, students may begin to suggest rules such as, "Do not steal pencils from other students. Do not write on other people's things. Always be nice to other students." While these are all great discussion points, especially coming from the perspective of the students, they are awfully specific. Lead your class in a discussion that these individual suggestions could all be combined into one effective rule, "Always treat your classmates and their property with respect." Once you have agreed on an overarching rule such as this, discuss or role-play through a few examples of what this looks like in the classroom. Once the rules are decided on, have the students suggest consequences for breaking them. You will be surprised by what the students come up with; help them to decide which suggestions are the fairest and most reasonable to put into place. Finally, have them record these rules on a poster board that can be displayed in the classroom for the remainder of the year. It is also nice to have the students sign the poster, either beneath the rules or by creating a border around them, to signify that they accept the rules and will work collectively to promote them.

You already have the necessary tools to increase students' autonomy by providing choice. Remember to use a standard to develop an assessment. Use the assessment to develop the lesson activities.

Because you understand the beginning (standard) and end (assessment) of the lesson, you can consider several different lesson activities that all accomplish the same goal. Provide students with a worksheet of options and allow them to choose which activities to engage in. Some teachers present these as a tic-tac-toe board or bingo board. Similarly, you could provide students with options for showing their learning through different assessment formats. Some may prefer to orally present information, while others prefer to make models, and still others prefer to write a story or essay incorporating their new knowledge.

During the lesson. New teachers may feel uncomfortable being in charge of their own classrooms for the first time and mistakenly consider classroom management as a way to "control" their students. Rather than attempting to control our students, we should be working to engage them in meaningful ways to support their learning. Self-determination theory demonstrates a clear connection between students' autonomy and intrinsic motivation (Ryan & Deci, 2000). Autonomy allows students some level of independence in the classroom while fostering a sense of ownership in their work. One of the most effective ways to provide students with this necessary autonomy is to build choice into the curriculum (Brooks & Young, 2011). You may build choice into the curriculum in order to allow students to pursue subjects of their own interests, to engage in learning tasks aligned with their learning styles, or to demonstrate their learning through preferred assessment formats. By providing students with this level of choice, they will be more likely to stay focused and interested in the lesson, reducing off-task behavior.

PLANNING PATHWAYS

Because you are most likely completing your edTPA in a classroom that is not your own, you may not have the ability to change many of the things discussed in this chapter. You should, however, still have control over the materials involved in the activities you are teaching as well as the level of cognitive challenge you provide in your lessons. Consider the learning segment you will submit in your portfolio and answer the following questions:

1   How will you organize your physical space and lesson materials?

2   How will you foster respectful student collaboration?

3   How will students engage in higher-order thinking?

4   Most importantly, how will these three things *be evident* in your video clips?

Don't expect your scorer to assume that you are doing these things; there must be evidence in the video clips that you have actually attended to each one of them. Take the time now to plan out how you can show all of these items in your video clips *and* how you can describe them in your commentary.

During the lesson, teachers must also continue to review expectations and model the type of behavior they want to see in their students. It is not enough to set classroom rules in the beginning of the school year. Instead, teachers must continually address students' concerns in a consistent way and assist students to do their best.

Summary

Your main goal in establishing a challenging learning environment within your classroom should be to build a safe and supportive class culture in which students are comfortable participating in the learning process and taking risks to deepen their own learning. This goal can be accomplished through the rapport you establish and promote within your class, the opportunities for critical thinking you provide your students, and the way you organize your classroom to facilitate student learning. Intentionally fostering student interactions will further support this goal as you ensure that students are respectful and collaborative. Using strategies discussed within this chapter will help you in your journey of developing a class culture that best supports student learning.

ORIENTATION
Where Are You Now?

1 What is constructivism, and how does it relate to your teaching?

2 Compare and contrast student-centered learning with student-driven learning. Provide an example of each.

3 Thinking of your particular students, write a short plan that you could use to facilitate student interactions.

CHAPTER 7

Using Assessment Data

You Are Here

You are gaining valuable experience in the field, developing engaging plans and implementing them effectively. You should also be recognizing the need for constant reflection in the teaching profession. Chapter 3 discussed planning effective assessments to gather data. These data are usually analyzed with student learning in mind. The counterpart to student learning is teaching effectiveness. While considering students' progress on measurable learning outcomes, you should also be thinking about how you taught the content and skills required by the students to reach the target level of learning. Are there changes you could have made?

This chapter will help you reflect on teaching practices and instructional decisions as they connect with student outcomes and future learning. Proposing supports for student learning and planning next steps for instruction based on assessment data will also be discussed.

Uses of Assessment Data

After you have planned and implemented your lessons, you will gather data through assessments—what you will use in Task 3. There are two main purposes for the Task 3 data analysis: (1) to analyze student learning and (2) to analyze your teaching effectiveness. These two purposes are certainly related, but they are not the same. In the first, you will be examining assessment data, searching for patterns of learning among your students; you will determine how well they *learned* the content and language you taught. In the second, you will be examining the data from the perspective of your own teaching practices; you will determine how well you *taught* the content and language. You might ask, "Well, if the students learned the content, doesn't that mean I taught it well? Why analyze both?" In some cases, this may be true, but it is not always the case. Evaluating your own effectiveness is taking your use of the data one step further. Once you have found patterns in student learning, you will be able to start determining which instructional strategies, tied to those patterns, were most (or least) effective with your students.

LANDMARK

You have probably already learned about metacognition through your theoretical foundations and/or psychology coursework. Metacognition is cognition *about* cognition; in other words, it is the thinking processes that allow students to examine their own thinking and learning (Woolfolk, 2007). Metacognition involves the students planning for their own learning, monitoring their learning, and evaluating their learning (Woolfolk, 2007). These processes allow students to consider what strategies are most beneficial to their learning and to consider changing plans when they find strategies to be ineffective.

You will be encouraging students' metacognitive processes by providing direct and specific feedback, which will allow them to consider what choices they made on the assessment, how they planned for studying, and how effectively they were monitoring and evaluating their own performance before the assessment to determine if changes will need to be made to their learning skill set.

Analysis of Student Learning

Analyzing student learning is the first step to determining how proficient your students have become and how well your teaching strategies have worked. *SCALE: For Rubric 11 of the edTPA, you will be examining your students' work in search of evidence that they have learned the skills and knowledge tied to your stated learning objectives.* It is important that you appropriately tied your assessment to your learning objective(s) back in the planning phase. If not, you may not actually be able to measure what your students learned with respect to the objective without using an additional assessment.

Depending on the type of assessment data you have collected, you may consider calculating class averages for each question as well as for the assessment as a whole. Similarly, you might consider separate parts of a writing assignment or project in addition to the assessment as a whole. Breaking down an assessment into smaller components will give you a better idea about your students' learning on each part rather than how they performed overall. This breakdown will reveal patterns of whole-class learning.

An example of analyzing data for student learning. Let's assume the project you are using as an assessment is an engineering design challenge. The knowledge and skills required to complete this type of assessment can be considered independently of one another. We can use the hypothetical data listed in table 7.1 as an example. The column to the right shows the students' overall grades for the project. These total scores are out of 100, while each category listed before them shows scores out of 20. If you were to calculate the class average, you would see that your students averaged an 83.5 percent, which, in most districts, is probably a B. You may take this as an indication that your students "did well" and move on. When you consider the *components* of the project, however, you will notice a different trend. The third column clearly shows that students struggled with identifying the criteria and constraints of their projects. You may also notice that the students were very successful at testing their solutions to the problem posed, as the class average in this category was close to a perfect score. It is this level of analysis that will allow you to determine the trends that exist in your whole-class data.

Notice that the categories along the top of table 7.1 relate to the *processes and skills* that students needed to use toward the final project. These are skills that you should highlight in your Task 1 learning-segment plans, showing how your instruction directly supports students' learning production. In your attempts to analyze student learning, you should be more focused on these critical processes and skills than you are on other measures such as word count, number of sentences per paragraph, and grammar and mechanics. These latter measures all have their place, but they are not direct measures of student learning; they are measures of other important academic skills. Here, discourse structure and disciplinary accuracy trump the finer points of grammar and mechanics.

When considering the edTPA, you will want to look for these patterns or trends in your data. Discuss what your students did well and what they struggled with, using evidence

Table 7.1. Mock Data for Engineering Design Project

Student #	Identifying a need	Considering criteria and constraints	Designing a solution	Testing the solution	Evaluating and revising solution	Overall grade
1	18	10	20	20	19	87
2	20	8	13	20	17	78
3	20	17	17	20	20	94
4	15	9	16	18	16	74
5	20	12	20	20	19	91
6	19	12	20	20	20	91
7	18	10	15	17	17	77
8	18	15	19	19	19	90
9	14	7	13	17	15	66
10	20	9	18	20	20	87
Class average	18.2	10.9	17.1	19.1	18.2	83.5

to support your claims. As you continue your teaching career, also continue these analyses. You may carefully construct project rubrics so that they reflect the main components of learning you would like to be able to assess separately. You can also explore digital assessment platforms that provide data-analysis tools so that you do not have to create spreadsheets like the one shown in table 7.1 on your own.

Focus students. Beyond whole-class data, you will need to choose three focus students. These students should represent three different types of learners in your class. For example, you may select an advanced student, an average student, and a student with a learning disability. Doing so will allow you to look at your assessment and resulting data from different perspectives. Similar to the preceding analysis, you may also consider trends for specific groups of students within your class. Did the English language learners in your class do poorly in one particular category? You can offer additional support in that area. Did your average students excel in another area? Be ready to provide greater challenges moving forward.

PLANNING PATHWAYS

Use the data in table 7.1 to write up a mock assessment commentary. Which three students would you suggest using as your focus students and why? How will you describe the learning that occurred in this classroom?

Providing feedback to learners. Teachers will often provide feedback to their students on their assessments. This is an important part of the practice. How often, as a student yourself, did you turn in an assignment to a professor and anxiously await to see how well you performed? Our own students feel the same way, and it is important for you to let them know how they are doing.

Feedback can come in several different forms. None of these forms, however, include check marks, *C*s across a paper, or *X*s and slashes through incorrect answers. These and similar marks only serve to differentiate between correct and incorrect responses without helping the students to understand why they were right or wrong. Research has shown such marks to be ineffective, and at times counterproductive, at helping students learn from their mistakes (Sadler, 1998). Feedback is meant to supplement instruction. It will allow students to continue learning by fostering metacognition. If the students look at what they got right or wrong on an assessment, along with your feedback to them, they can start to reconsider their own thinking processes that led to incorrect conclusions (Hattie, 2011). *SCALE: Rubric 12 assesses your ability to provide feedback to your students.* Feedback will be most effective, and therefore earn you the highest score, when you address students' strengths, weaknesses, and a recommended learning strategy for improvement. Personal and individually tailored comments can be made by addressing what you know of your students' individual assets and prior learning (Sadler, 1998).

Acceptable forms of feedback might include comments written directly on the assessment, a separate feedback page, or oral feedback. All of these options offer specific information that your students can incorporate into their learning. In each case, you are tailoring your comments to the specific strengths and/or weaknesses of your students. In this individualized way, your feedback will be more meaningful to your students.

Some teachers write comments directly onto their students' papers so that the feedback is connected to students' responses in an obvious way. This may be a good choice when students have had to draw, diagram, or show work to support their responses. A related approach is to use sticky notes so that you can write more on the page, especially if the student's work takes up a majority of the blank space.

Alternatively, a separate feedback page can be returned with the students' original assessment papers. On this separate page, teachers will often write summaries of what students have done well, what students still need to work on, and/or a plan for further development. Though this technique might be useful in many situations, it is especially useful for assessments that indicate patterns of strength or weakness, such as long writing assignments with numerous punctuation errors or math tests with many subtraction errors. If you notice that your student makes the same mistake over and over again, it may be more harmful to them to have you write across the paper for every mistake. In this instance, you should opt for a separate feedback page that reviews the student's particular area of weakness (i.e., long division) so that you are supporting the student's continued learning without taking away their motivation and sense of confidence.

Finally, oral feedback is also an acceptable way to let students know how they are doing. Much like the written forms, however, it is most effective when done individually for each student. Some teachers set up miniconferences with students to discuss their progress toward learning goals. The benefit to these conferences is that they allow students to ask questions and take part in the process with the teacher. For the purposes of the edTPA, such conferences can be audio or video recorded and shared as the uploaded evidence of feedback.

SCENIC DETOUR

Grading Convention and ESL Students

There are many procedures that occur in a US classroom that teachers often take for granted. These procedures are best seen in daily routines. In an elementary setting, this might include the Pledge of Allegiance, a morning meeting, and set times for students to go to their "specials." In a secondary school, it often consists of homeroom and following a set schedule of different classes throughout the day. Even these classes have embedded routines and structures within them. Perhaps teachers expect homework to be turned in to a designated bin in the classroom. Asking permission to use the restroom may be done through its own set of conventions such as raising your hand, signing a log sheet, or taking a hall pass. New and immigrant students have a lot to learn about the hidden curriculum of US classrooms, even if they already know how to speak English (Parkay, 2016). The set of grading conventions the teachers in the United States often use is no exception.

In many countries in the Middle East, it is traditional to use the letter *X* as shorthand to stand for Christ. In certain dialects of languages such as Greek, Turkish, and Armenian, this shorthand symbol is used often and will appear in a lot of English translations. This explains why you may have seen "Merry X-mas" at some point in your life.

In the United States, many teachers use the letter *X* to mark problems as incorrect. I once had an Armenian student share with me that her cousin, who was new to US schools, was terribly confused when she started receiving papers back from her teacher. These papers were covered in a series of *X*s. She then asked her cousin, who was older and had grown up in the United States, why the teacher would keep writing "Christ, Christ, Christ" all over her answers.

This vignette is meant to demonstrate two ideas. First, a student will not continue to learn when you simply mark answers as right or wrong. Second, it is important to teach our immigrant students about our educational system in addition to the subject matter and language we hope to teach them.

Learners' use of feedback. Providing feedback to students is only one piece of the puzzle. You cannot assume that students will know what to do with the feedback once it is given. Instead, "students should also be trained in how to interpret feedback, how to make connections between the feedback and the characteristics of the work they produce, and how they can improve their work in the future" (Sadler, 1998, p. 77). Help students to understand and use the feedback you have provided to them so that they may continue to learn through the assessment process. To do this, you can build some routines and structures into your typical classroom management system, especially following an assessment.

One way to help your students following an assessment is to conference with them individually or in small groups of students with similar needs. You can guide them through a discussion of what went well and what they struggled with. Ask them probing questions and allow them to ask questions of you too. You may also work together to identify goals for learning and plan next steps toward those goals together.

Some teachers take a different approach and require students to correct answers on a test or correct their writing on an essay and resubmit for additional points. This approach is beneficial when used properly because it does allow for metacognition and students' building on their own previous understanding and skills. As the teacher, however, you have to be sure to provide additional support to help the students before they resubmit the assignment. How could you possibly expect them to turn it back in (and suddenly have the right answers) if you haven't retaught the concepts using alternate strategies? Focus on providing supports in the areas of students' weakness so that this option is attainable for you and for your students.

As in the case of the class shown in table 7.1, you may also consider applying a whole-class intervention for a specific weakness shown through assessment data. In the table, students mainly struggled with identifying criteria and constraints. To help the students understand the feedback you have given them, you may want to orally review your feedback with the whole class before providing additional instruction on the topic. Use different teaching methods than you had originally and provide more support in an attempt to reach more students in your class.

Though these suggestions are not the only ways you might consider using feedback in your classroom, they should provide insight into the process. You will need to develop strategies that work best for you and for your students. Your main goals should be helping students to recognize patterns in their own learning and helping them to build toward greater levels of achievement.

Analysis of Teaching Effectiveness

The first use of student assessment data was surely to determine how well the students understood the content, applied the skills, and used the language you had taught them. These data, and your analysis of them thus far, will help you to analyze the effectiveness of your instruction. Common practice for teachers is to begin this process through reflection on instructional implementation (Task 2) and the use of local, formative assessment data (Task 3). Once you have considered these data sets, you will be able to propose supports for your students' continued development in addition to planning your next steps of instruction.

Reflection. Research on reflective practices in teaching abound (Ottesen, 2007). This type of reflection has taken various forms and been used for similarly numerous purposes. When you reflect on your teaching practices, you probably do so by asking yourself (or having a supervisor or cooperating teacher ask you) a few questions. The two questions you will probably hear most often are, "How do you think that went?" and

"What would you have done differently?" Answers to these questions will routinely focus on classroom management. Though we have already discussed the importance of classroom management and its potential impact on learning, this form of shortsighted reflection fails to fully consider how your teaching has translated to student learning. These questions and answers discussed during post-observation conferences or through written reflections on your own lesson plans will not be as helpful to guiding your future instruction as will be the consideration of specific teaching techniques and their effectiveness.

The form of reflection you engage in can vary. It may be a reflection with your cooperating teacher after a lesson, a discussion of your lesson with a clinical supervisor after an observation, a required written piece added to each lesson plan, or simply something you consider independently. If you find that you are not required to discuss your lesson afterward with an experienced professional, nor are you responsible for writing out reflections on your plans, you should still make a point to reflect independently. It is yet another habit you must build as an educator. Why spend the time and energy planning dynamic lessons if they don't actually accomplish the goals you've planned for your students? You must continually work to understand how well you have done as an educator so you can continue making improvements in your instruction that ultimately improve your students' learning.

Figure 7.1 provides examples of the types of questions and answers you may encounter in the reflective process. The first two columns include examples of the questions and responses you may typically hear teachers ask and answer about their own teaching. These are especially true for novice teachers and teacher candidates who have a greater concern for developing "control" over their classrooms. Similarly, these are the

Common reflective questions	Common answers	What you should really be thinking
• How did that lesson go? • What could I have done differently? • What would have helped the students understand _____ better? • How did the students do on that assignment?	• "It went pretty well but..." • "I should have spoken up more so the students in the back could hear me better." • "Next time, I need to give better instructions. The students seemed confused when they started the activity." • "Most of the students did fine on the project. They mostly got A's."	• Did I differentiate enough to meet the various learning needs of my students? • Did my assessment really capture the learning goal in the way I intended? • Did I provide enough scaffolds to support my students to reach the objective? • Could I have altered my teaching strategy or activity to better teach this lesson? • Was my lesson appropriately student-centered and student-driven?

Figure 7.1. Reflective questions and answers

types of responses teacher candidates may plan to discuss in their edTPA assessment commentaries. The third column provides alternate questions to consider when reflecting on your practice. Notice that there is nothing "wrong" with the questions and answers provided in the first two columns. The problem is mainly that they relate to classroom management alone and don't tell the whole story of your overall teaching effectiveness.

For the purposes of your edTPA and for your teaching career afterward, you should develop a habit of asking questions more like those found in the third column of figure 7.1. These questions challenge you to think more deeply about how you taught the lesson rather than simply how you handled the students during the lesson. You might consider differentiation, instructional approaches, scaffolding techniques, assessment alignment, and so on.

PLANNING PATHWAYS

It's time to reflect on your reflections. After teaching your next lesson, work independently or with your cooperating teacher to reflect on the lesson's effectiveness. How many of the questions you discussed are similar to those in the first column of figure 7.1? How many are similar to those in the third column? If you didn't consider some of the third-column topics, reflect on them now.

Using local, formative data. In chapters 2 and 3, we discussed different forms of assessment. Each assessment type serves a different purpose. For the purposes of analyzing teaching effectiveness and planning your next steps of instruction, you should concentrate on data from local, formative assessments and local, summative assessments. These local assessments are the ones created by you and are therefore aligned to your class's individual learning goals. This alignment is what will allow you to think critically about your students' progress toward your stated goals and how you supported this progress. These data will allow you to check for students' understanding throughout and across lessons.

Using critical reflection, coupled with an analysis of student performance data, allows you to recognize some areas of your teaching that should be further developed to continue to allow for student growth. It is imperative that you recognize that your teaching does not conclude with a unit test; in reality, any assessment that you give should be carefully analyzed for student comprehension. Using data or results from your students' performance on these local assessments will reveal areas of strength and weakness. Earlier, we discussed what that means with regard to student learning. Here, we are challenging you to take the patterns you identify in the data once step further; identifying strengths and weaknesses in student performance may indicate strengths and weaknesses in your own performance.

An example of analyzing data for teacher performance. If you are teaching your students to calculate the area of irregularly shaped objects, the students will need to understand (1) how area is calculated, (2) how to multiply, (3) how to identify the length and width of an object, and (4) how to break the larger irregular object down into smaller, regular shapes when needed. As you evaluate your students' assessment responses, you may see that almost all of your students are able to find the area of regular rectangles, find the length and width of these objects, and multiply with few errors. That's great! What is it you did to teach these concepts? Identify what works so that you can keep on using these strategies. You may also have found a pattern where the students seem unable to break down a larger irregular object into regular shapes. This is an area that you will need to reteach. What strategies have you tried already? There are many reasons why these strategies may have been unsuccessful. You may even notice that these strategies worked well with one group of students but completely missed the mark with another group. That's okay; every student (and class of students) engages in content and strategy differently. What you need to do is consider how to help the students who did not understand the content the first time you taught the unit.

Proposing supports. You have carefully reflected on your own practices and looked through your student data. **SCALE: *These data sources should reveal to you patterns in whole-class learning, a vital component of Rubric 11.*** So what do you do with this information?

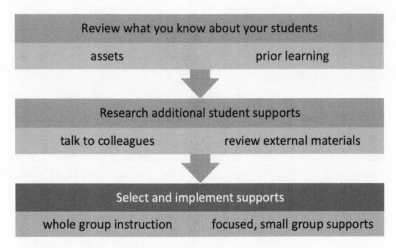

Figure 7.2. Suggested activities to follow assessment analysis

The unit is over, so you should introduce a new topic, right? Wrong. Once you have identified areas of weakness, you will need to propose supports for your students. Some of your initial strategies probably didn't work with a particular set of students. The flow chart in figure 7.2 offers suggestions as to what you do next.

You will need to reconsider your students with regard to the assets and prior learning they bring into the classroom. Think about their strengths and weaknesses in the learning process and what tends to motivate them. Then, you should look into alternate strategies and additional supports. The plan you used originally wasn't the best fit for them. Do you already have another plan that you think would be better suited to their needs? If so, try it. If not, you should have professional conversations with colleagues. Other experienced teachers within your school may have had success using different techniques that you could try. Professional associations and organizations also provide support in the form of resources, journals, lesson plans or activities, and a network of teachers just like you who teach in similar content areas or grades levels. You may also find resources or ideas for lessons using your teacher's edition of your textbook or online. Finally, you select the strategies that you think will best meet the needs of your learners and implement them. This could be in the form of whole-class instruction, if you believe it would benefit many of the students in your class, or small-group instruction, if you believe there are a few target students needing assistance.

LANDMARK

Many teacher preparation programs require candidates to complete professional portfolios. While there may be some variety in the standards to which candidates must respond, most portfolios reveal five common themes across their standards:

1 Knowledge of students

2 Knowledge of content

3 Instructional skills

4 Assessment skills

5 Development as a professional

These themes are so common that the edTPA includes the first four themes as a function of the assessment.

As you think about and plan additional instructional supports, be sure to document your conversations with colleagues. One way to meet new colleagues and to gain a broader picture of content instruction is through professional associations called SPAs (specialized professional associations). You should consider joining a professional association like the National Council for the Social Studies (NCSS), the National Council of Teachers of Mathematics (NCTM), the National Science Teaching Association (NSTA), the National Council of Teachers of English (NCTE), or the American Council on the Teaching of Foreign Languages (ACTFL).

Membership in these organizations, and documentation of specific work with colleagues, can be used in your professional portfolio. Principals want to hire engaged, collaborative faculty. Your demonstrated abilities to learn with and from colleagues will help you be a better teacher and land that job you're looking for!

Though you have now completed the flow chart outlined in figure 7.2, your work is not done. As you should have noticed already, the processes of planning, implementing, and assessing are cyclical. You have implemented support strategies to assist students in the areas of weakness you identified through an assessment. Only through the analysis of additional formative assessment data will you be able to determine whether your new attempts have worked. Figure 7.3 demonstrates the cyclical nature of the teaching processes.

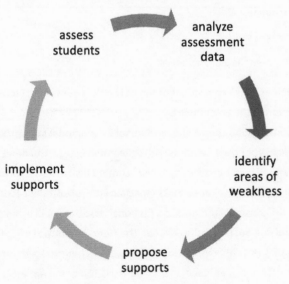

Figure 7.3. The cyclical nature of teaching processes

Planning next steps in instruction. While the edTPA only requires you to complete one learning segment (and a whole lot of writing!), the teaching profession requires you to consistently learn from your students, employing the best instructional strategies to guide students to deeper learning. You can turn your edTPA into an artifact for your professional portfolio by completing at least one cycle of the teaching process (figure 7.3). Meet with colleagues, attend a professional conference (your principal or your school of education might even help pay for it), or read scholarly works about your discipline. When your research is done, propose and implement a new support to address areas of weakness. Is this more work than just moving to the next chapter in the textbook? Yes. Will it pay dividends when your students are able to understand the concepts and skills behind what you are teaching? Absolutely! Take the next step after the edTPA and be the teacher who really cares about student learning.

Summary

In this chapter, we explored the components of analyzing data (1) for student learning and (2) for teaching effectiveness. The edTPA requires candidates to assess student work samples for student learning, sharing student work samples and aggregate student data (see table 7.1). Analyzing student work in this way and reflecting critically on your own teaching practices is difficult work, but it will help you to "teach like a pro" (Hargreaves & Fullan, 2012) and best support student learning and the profession at large. As you gain experience, it will become a normal part of your routine, and you will see your students benefit in the process.

ORIENTATION

Where Are You Now?

1 How is using assessment to analyze student learning similar to and different from using assessment to inform instruction?

2 Why is feedback such an important part of the teaching process?

3 Use the flow chart depicted in figure 7.2 after analyzing the data from your next assessment. Try implementing a new technique to reach a greater number of learners in your class, and describe how effective the new technique was.

CHAPTER 8

New Frontiers in Teacher Performance Assessments

ORIENTATION

You Are Here

When you picked up this book, you were interested in the edTPA, the performance assessment you are currently facing. But as chapter 1 noted, performance assessments are not new to education, nor are they new to teacher preparation. Over the decades, teachers, teacher educators, and administrators have collaboratively explored ways to best prepare preservice, novice, and veteran teachers for different contextual challenges that face schools, students, and communities. Over the past two decades, the increasing prevalence of technology in instruction and assessment (if those two things are thought to be separate) has added a new dimension to teacher performance assessments.

This chapter is future facing. It calls us all to reflect on the ways that we might be able to (whether we are willing to or not) assess teacher performance. These methods, techniques, and models are not currently tied to any particular platform; these ideas are all under development. They are important because they could impact your tenure or posttenure reviews, just as the edTPA has impacted your certification program. Let's look now at how the landscape we have mapped out may be shifting.

Small Data, Big Results

Throughout your edTPA process, you have generated a lot of data. Prior to even beginning this process, your assignments generated student data that led you to develop your learning segment. Your learning-segment assessments generated more data, aligned with the checks for understanding, exit slips, and formative classwork assessments that you included throughout your learning segment. You also generated personal data in the form of your lesson plans, Task 2 videos, and commentaries.

While these are a lot of data, they are (comparatively) "small" data. The data that you and your students generated are specific to the context of your school, your classroom, your instruction, and your students' representations of learning. These data are different from the "big" data aggregated by smart machine algorithms that find disparate predictive connections across a wide array of contexts. While there is certainly some marketable use for such big data crunching—this may be the understatement of the century—it is in small data use that person-to-person, humanistic educational experiences thrive.

In a way, teachers are expert purveyors of small data. In chapter 1, we discussed the role of teacher performance assessments to serve as indicators for "good" and/or "effective" teaching. The philosophical premise that underlies such work is that in order to be a good and effective teacher, one must know their students to such a degree that they can provide an appropriately challenging education to each student. This is a premise on which educational philosophers and theorists have agreed for centuries. From Dewey's (1916, 1938) educative experiences for democratic development to Montessori's (1965) "prepared/enabling environments," to Vygotsky's (1978) "zone of proximal development" (ZPD), scholars agree that teachers need to know where their students are before they can design educational programs to develop their capacities for the future. Knowing "where students are" requires teachers to be judicious, intentional collectors and analyzers of student data.

Current and future performance assessments are sure to develop more sophisticated measures of teacher candidates' and teachers' abilities to systematically collect student data, analyze it, and use that analysis to support student learning needs and goals. The edTPA as a whole (and Task 3 in particular) demonstrates this trend. Through written reflection, the edTPA really assesses a candidate's ability to collect, analyze, and use student data from the beginning of the assessment to the end. Thus, when we organized this book, we discussed *assessment* in two places:

1   In chapter 3, we focused on developing a summative assessment that not only drove your learning-segment design but also served as the final assessment for the learning segment.

2   In chapter 7, we focused on how to analyze data from that summative assessment, not in superficial terms (e.g., did students use correct grammar and include "the right" number of sentences), but in terms of concepts and skills taught across the learning segment.

Assessment is the driver of the edTPA.

While teachers work with small data every day, and the edTPA asks for you to do the same, companies and organizations with big data capabilities are exploring ways to make use of such data. This chapter explores what some of those possibilities look like, drawing on the rapid rise of big data educational capabilities throughout the K–12 school system. In many instances, what is discussed in the rest of this chapter is morally, ethically, and philosophically neutral. But, as we shift from small to big data use, there is a shift from local data control (at the level of the teacher, principal, and school district) to national or corporate control, increasing the power of the data. It is wise, therefore, that we remember the Peter Parker Principle—with great power comes great responsibility!

The Rise of Small Data: Infotech in Education

Not long ago, small data ubiquitously lived in the paper gradebooks of teachers throughout the world. As students turned in their assignments (written on paper), teachers would provide feedback (written on paper), score the work, and return it to the students. The hope was that the students would apply the feedback on their next assignments, but it was just as likely that the students would throw it out or lose it in their lockers along with their gym socks and half-eaten sandwiches.

Today, more than half the U.S. student population (30 million of the 56.6 million elementary and secondary students) uses at least one Google suite app to support their learning (Singer, 2017). In addition to app use, Google also has a large share of Chromebooks in U.S. schools that allow for teachers to augment the integrated technology experience across students (users) in a class (Taylor, 2015). Those data are stored with Google, increasing the ability for them to be mined and used in increasingly creative ways.

The potential for big data collection and uses with school information (e.g., users' age, gender, assignment completion, and performance) is a symptom of the widespread use of data throughout the country. When discussing the role of technology in schools, some people are quick to criticize the use of smart devices and computers for instruction—right before they pick up their own phones to use an app! "As it becomes more commonplace for children to use mobile devices at home, it will be a natural progression to accept personal device use in the classroom. It should not surprise us that more school districts are adopting personal device programs" (Moon, 2018, p. 294). The same demographic information that is collected on students' personal lives is also collected on their school lives. Educators have long discussed breaking down the walls of the school to provide educative experiences for students; in many ways, technology integration has done just that.

But while we assess the ways in which student data can and should be used (and by whom), we also need to consider the ways that the use of such technologies in the classroom will impact the ways teacher candidates and teachers are assessed. We also need to explore the ways that data are being used to assess teachers' instructional decision-making. The information that technology applications are collecting on both teacher pedagogy and teacher instructional decision-making may impact teacher performance assessment in the near future.

Assessing How Teachers Use Technologies

It is no secret that internet-based technologies are expanding around the world. "Technological growth is such that by 2025, 90% of the world's population will be using media devices to connect to the internet" (World Economic Forum, 2017). The speed at which these changes continue to grow is directly impacting the ways in which teachers choose to develop instructional activities (Moon, 2018) and the ways that schools are conceiving of a twenty-first-century learning environment (November, 2012).

One of the pressing issues with the increased integration of technology in classrooms is the role of expert knowledge—from the typical "knower" (the teacher) to the typically high-frequency technology consumer (the student). As Alan November (2012) illustrates, technology is blurring the lines between knower and learner and between what it means to be a digital native in context. For example, knowing how to create, edit, and post images online is an important skill. So is knowing how to effectively use data-analysis software. But these two skills are not comparable, nor do they create an efficient, scalable curriculum model. As separate skills, both need to be taught for students to appropriately harness the power of digital learning.

Who *Knows* the Technology?

While digital natives and digital immigrants may understand and use technology differently, there is a research effect that is important to explore. Many of the studies of how students and teachers engage with technology are conducted via self-assessments (Kaarakainen, Kivinen, & Vainio, 2018). Oftentimes, these self-assessment surveys are unreliable; people either over- or underestimate their abilities with information and communications technology (ICT). For example, an adolescent who views herself to be a savvy digital native is likely to overestimate her abilities to navigate complex HTML-based programming software. On the other hand, adults who have learned (or been told) that they do not have the skills required to work statistical software might underestimate their abilities to perform tasks in other software domains.

An alternative to these self-assessment measures are task-based assessments, in which participants demonstrate their abilities to complete certain tasks using the technology provided in the classroom. These measures are less frequently used because they require a good deal of time and attention to evaluate participants' performance. Such studies demonstrate both the breadth and depth of technology use across participant groups, however, leading to interesting findings about technology proficiency.

For example, Meri-Tuulia Kaarakainen and her colleagues (2018) conducted a study of ICT skill assessment with 3,159 students and 629 teachers in Finland, exploring basic digital skills, advanced technological skills (e.g., software installation and maintenance tasks), and professional ICT skills (e.g., ICT skills needed for higher-education contexts). Their study showed that both students and teachers were proficient at basic digital skills but that there was a teacher-student divide related to advanced technological skills and professional ICT skills. Interestingly, students were found to have better proficiency at the professional ICT skills than the teacher participants!

LANDMARK

Harvard professor Tony Wagner (2008) asked business leaders to describe the types of skills high school graduates would need to be successful. The following seven themes emerged from their answers:

1 Critical Thinking and Problem Solving

2 Collaboration and Leading by Influence

3 Agility and Adaptability

4 Initiative and Entrepreneurialism

5 Effective Oral and Written Communication

6 Accessing and Analyzing Information

7 Curiosity and Imagination

These skills were probably discussed in your program when discussing twenty-first-century education. They are not equal, though. Cal Newport (2016) argues that only the skills that are rare and require a deep understanding of underlying concepts are the most valuable—rewarded with both money and status. His research concludes that the skill of accessing and analyzing complex sets of information is more valuable now and in the future. Whereas the YouTube star is a real phenomenon, instances of such stardom are rare. Teaching students to do the deep work of analysis might serve our students better.

As 1:1 computing devices proliferate across school districts, next-generation curriculum is developed, and more teachers integrate technology into their instruction (either through will or by force), there will be an increased need to assess teachers' abilities to perform the types of professional tasks that they will need to teach students. These skills will extend beyond the role of technology for communication and collaboration, focusing instead on the role of technology for accessing and analyzing information.

Evaluating teachers' abilities to access and analyze information through various qualitative and quantitative software would be a logical next step to assess pre-service and in-service teacher preparation. Digital task assessments would provide similar information to content-area exams already taken by pre-service teachers throughout the country. Tied with the competency-based assessments explored shortly, these assessments would not evaluate knowledge that can be easily found with a search engine. Rather, they would evaluate the extent to which teachers are able to perform the tasks that we increasingly need our students to complete in a competitive, technologically dependent economy.

Assessment Literacy in the Digital Age

While knowing what to teach is important, knowing how to assess student work and provide formative feedback that drives future instruction and changes in student learning have become even more critical topics (Black & Wiliam, 1998). Effective formative feedback raises the probability that a student will learn more than a student without effective feedback by 90 percent (Hattie, 2011). If the student can effectively (accurately) self-report grades and expectations on an assignment, that probability raises 144 percent. These two practices raise the probability of positive learning outcomes for every child in a class where they are practiced!

In order to implement these assessment practices, though, teachers need *assessment literacy*. There are two ways that we can think of assessment literacy. The first focuses on teachers' abilities to develop appropriate assessments for their students. In large part, this type of assessment literacy is what the edTPA examines. By asking you to develop an assessment related to your learning segment, edTPA evaluators can examine the ways in which you are able to backward-design instruction using instructional standards, mastery objectives, and related disciplinary skills.

The second way that we can think of assessment literacy is related to teachers' understanding and abilities to collect the data that are most useful for improving student learning. To an extent, the edTPA also focuses on this aspect of assessment literacy. In Task 3, you are asked to develop a rubric connected to your summative assessment. Thinking back to your rubric, you probably left off items such as "proper grammar" and "each paragraph has five sentences." These are formatting items that do not directly assess student performance relative to your learning goals.

With the rise in 1:1 digital device integration in classrooms across the country, the role of teachers in selecting the data that best support student learning is even more critical. The 1:1 instructional device ratio allows students to engage in content and assignments asynchronously. Students now have the opportunity to extend their learning time to engage in more thoughtful disciplinary communication. Liat Eyal (2012) argues that as digital technologies increasingly give students power to self-regulate and be reflective learners, the teacher's ability to provide clear metrics for educational success, thoughtful data-selection criteria, and clear analysis become more important instructional skills than in the past.[*]

Assessing Teacher Performance in Digital Classrooms

As the market for and implementation of digital instruction increases, either in its hybrid form or in its purely virtual form, performance assessments like the edTPA will have to evolve to flexibly incorporate various instructional models to fit rubric guidelines. Before COVID-19 caused mass closures of schools around the country, the edTPA implicitly defined instructional implementation within the scope of a traditional,

---

[*] During the 2020 COVID-19 pandemic, many schools closed, and student teachers were forced to complete their student teaching experiences online. The edTPA provided alternate guidance for those candidates to complete their edTPA portfolio. All of the tasks and rubrics remained the same; the only change in 2020 was related to the types of evidence one could provide (e.g., email communications with students). We argue here that the edTPA may be revised to evaluate candidates' assessment literacy, something that it does not currently do.

synchronous classroom experience. While the prompts could theoretically be applied to various styles of online learning (either synchronous or asynchronous), the action steps that candidates needed to take to engage in Task 2 all suggested that candidates needed to be in the same physical location as their students. By providing directions about consent forms, camera angles, and other general tips for recording instruction, the edTPA assumed candidates would be teaching students a certain way. As school districts quickly implemented remote learning plans to deal with the pandemic, Pearson (the company responsible for edTPA implementation) reactively had to make changes to the types of materials student teachers could submit in their portfolios. As we have discussed to this point, asynchronous learning may be a larger part of future education and therefore require other measures to capture teacher progress.

SCENIC DETOUR

The Influence of Instructional Design on Education

In contrast to the teacher preparation and certification work that traditional teacher preparation programs provide (e.g., education courses, scaffolded professional field experiences, and student teaching), instructional design programs enable students to learn curriculum, design, and assessment theory. Rather than working in face-to-face classrooms, instructional/curriculum designers often work in online settings. In these online settings, designers build, manage, and assess student learning, creating virtual classroom environments.

The work of Salmon Khan, while not an instructional designer by training, is a good example of what instructional designers do. Khan is the creator of Khan Academy, the popular online tutorial website. The website offers materials (in this case, video explanations of common K–12 concepts) to help people learn information. Most instructional designers work in fields other than K–12 education. They may work in business to create online trainings, for example. Today, however, instructional designers are slowly becoming important contributors to the K–12 learning space, where they craft materials for students and teachers.

Exploring the need for a more robust framework to evaluate online instruction in media-rich environments (much like the ones that Alan November [2012] describes with his idea of a "digital learning farm"), Jorge Reyna and Peter Meier (2018) have developed a framework for planning, implementing, and assessing learner-generated digital media (LGDM). LGDM is an all-encompassing term used for digital products that students can create to both learn and demonstrate their learning. For example, think of all of the teachers you know experimenting with students demonstrating their knowledge of content via Flipgrid, TikTok, and other social media outlets. Whether these products and outlets are geared toward everyday or professional ICT skills (Kaarakainen et al., 2018), such digital product planning, development, hosting, and evaluation are requisite skills for such assignments.

To that end, Reyna and Meier (2018) developed an eight-step model, outlining the process of planning, implementing, and assessing digital products. When paired side by side with the edTPA model (see table 8.1), distinct similarities are immediately recognizable. In both models, teachers are expected to forefront pedagogical decisions, linking and aligning student learning activities to disciplinary standards and learning objectives. Learning is also viewed as a social process; students in both models are expected to collaborate in authentic ways, codeveloping instruction. Finally, both models expect some form of feedback, reflection, and evaluation. Learning, then,

Table 8.1. A Comparison of the edTPA and the Learner-Generated Digital Media (LGDM) Models

The edTPA model	The LGDM model
Planning Pedagogic decisions center on a summative assessment of the teacher's choosing. Three- to five-lesson learning segment is scaffolded to achieve student success. Learning activities are related to that scaffolded approach.	**Preparing** Pedagogic decisions center on summative digital media product and method of student interaction. Some set of instructional materials are used to teach the content. Some set of training materials are used to support student digital product creation. Some set of materials are used to support student hosting of digital products.
Implementing One-to-two videos of direct instruction with students are prepared. There is a focus on academic language and subject-specific pedagogy.	**Representing** Time and attention are given to the complexity of the digital product in terms of weighted percentage and rubric development. Students are expected to create and publish digital products. Instructional feedback and student collaboration are moderated throughout the process—sometimes using online programs.
Assessing Feedback is provided at the duration of the learning segment on the basis of assessment performance. There is a focus on three student work samples Aggregate class data are used. The teacher is the final evaluator.	**Reinforcing** Feedback is consistent through the entirety of product development. Student reflection on their learning is a product of the feedback provided. The teacher is the final evaluator.

is viewed in both models as a constructivist activity, engaging students in the ongoing process of disciplinary ways of thinking and communicating.

However, rather than focusing on planning, implementing, and assessing, Reyna and Meier's (2018) LGDM model views learning through digital media through three different steps—"preparing, representing, and reinforcing" (p. 2). It is interesting to note that these steps (and this model as a whole) refocus the analysis from instruction to learning. In doing so, the model assumes that students are developing artifacts of their learning and that those artifacts are crafted in a learning environment supported by the teacher. In other words, the LGDM model is student centered rather than teacher centered. This shift focuses not on what the teacher does but on what the teacher enables the students to do.

Outcomes of this shift can be found in the subset of activities that blur the boundaries between planning, instruction, and assessment. For example, student training and hosting videos are important pieces for teachers to plan in order to help students effectively use and publish digital products. These are both part of the planning and instructional processes. Related to that instructional process is the collaborative, open-source feel of predesigned group contribution, feedback, and reflection. These four components are embedded into the instructional model prior to evaluation, enabling students to collaborate and problem-solve prior to publishing what will be evaluated not just by the teacher but, potentially, by the whole world. This model assumes that teachers and students are friendly critics, mentors, and coaches, all capable of providing useful feedback to each other. In this case, the teacher (with evaluation power) becomes "first among equals" in providing instructional supports and feedback on digital learning products.

It is also important to note that the LGDM model is intended to facilitate digital media instruction across multiple weeks. Unlike the edTPA, which is completed across three-to-five lessons, there is a recognition in the LGDM model that authentic instructional products take a long time to produce—be they digital or analog. The LGDM model extends the theoretical assessment parameters of the edTPA to include instruction over longer periods of time.

Using Students' Digital Work to Assess Teacher Performance

Current teacher performance assessments, like the edTPA, focus on teachers' abilities to develop students' disciplinary ways of thinking and communicating. State learning standards align to this goal, mainly focusing on building students' capacities to construct traditional academic genres (e.g., recount, explanation, and argument). Digital instruction, however, opens new, interconnected ways of thinking that merge and redefine disciplinary communication. While technology is not necessary for such instructional innovation (see the example of Finland's recent curriculum developments [Spiller, 2017]), networked devices, collaborative software, and social media platforms are clearly driving forces for such approaches.

As traditional and online learning become more widespread and mutually supportive, it will become more important to assess teachers' abilities not only to teach digital literacies but also to assess their abilities to design, employ, manage, and assess online asynchronous learning. In the context of the edTPA, that might look like a summative assessment that engages students in the digital production of a disciplinary product. In the context of tenure packets, that might look like a portfolio of student work and the metrics by which those projects are successful for their purposes. In either case, it is becoming clearer that student work will be a focus of assessment equal to, if not more important than, lesson-plan design. As the LGDM model demonstrates, the preparation for such work is less of a linear set of learning activities directed by the teacher and more of a puzzle-project variously and differently used by students, building materials that together form a coherent learning experience toward students' digital products.

There is a cautionary note here, however. The metrics by which the field defines "success" for various teacher performance assessments at the pre-service and novice levels will shift the values of instruction. Two hypothetical examples mark this point:

1 There could be a world in which students' digital projects are defined as "successful" and their learning deemed "satisfactory" by virtue of their ability to use existing software to convey ideas. In this sense, the summative assessments used in the edTPA would not be dissimilar to those used in this "new" assessment. The "new" assessment would just be a digitally augmented version of the traditional summative assessment.

2 There could also be a world where students' digital projects are defined as "successful" and their learning deemed "satisfactory" by virtue of their ability to garner views, likes, hearts, or whatever badging system a particular social media platform uses. Such a system might offer a more authentic version of success in the social media sphere, drawing on the goals of twenty-first-century learning (Wagner, 2012).

In these two hypothetical worlds, the "rules of the game" are drastically different, and the implications of these decisions would have real-world impacts on teachers and students.

The extent to which the field allows the gamified realities of social media to drive the definition of successful learning could alter the ways in which students comprehend, challenge, and engage in thoughtful scholarship. The extent to which the field accepts these parameters would also have a profound impact on the successful demonstration of teaching, as both current practice and theoretical models assume that teaching and learning performance are interconnected.

Privatization of Teacher Performance Assessments

As anyone who has been in the classroom within the past twenty years can attest, the privatization of education is a real phenomenon. Among the products of this privatization are the standardized tests and curricula that psychometric contracting companies create for use in the classroom. The stakes are high for such companies; contracts can extend to the tens of millions of dollars over periods of five or more years (see Decker [2015] for detailed information about the Pearson-Questar battle for New York State funds). Complete with prescriptive curriculum books and activities, such contracts embed private testing organizations into the lived experiences of students and teachers. The edTPA is an example of such privatization.

Currently, such privatization is checked by states' control of education. In order for curriculum, assessment, and some instructional materials (e.g., textbooks and intervention programs) to be adopted in schools, most states require that they be approved by state or local boards of education. Regarding teacher performance assessments, there are emerging technologies that have the potential both to be more useful to school administrators than many of the current educational products (e.g., the edTPA) and to require less oversight from state authorities (e.g., open systems that are not packaged products), increasing the privatized nature of teacher assessment. In particular, badging and virtual-reality experiences are emerging as areas for teacher performance assessment, tied to the standards created to assess teacher performance.

Badging as a Form of Credentialing

In 2009, the Gates Foundation, with its admirable quest to provide better instruction to low-income students, had an idea. Together with then–secretary of education Arne Duncan, the Gates Foundation began its Measures of Effective Teaching (MET) project (Bill & Melinda Gates Foundation, n.d.). Using standardized test scores and teaching observations as measurement tools, the project set the ambitious agenda to identify the critical attributes of good teaching. If those attributes could be identified, the thinking went, then we could tell who the good teachers were and usher out or train up the rest.

While the overall project, with its half-billion-dollar price tag, was a failure (Strauss, 2018), a teacher observation tool was developed that promised to provide comparable metrics of teacher performance. This tool is the Danielson Framework for Teaching (2011 Revised Edition) (Teachscape, 2011). The tool was used in the MET project and revised based on lessons learned in the first two years of the project's implementation. With this tool, states such as New York were able to assess their teachers' performance more accurately than before, putting a number to teacher performance using various indicators and giving principals and supervisors access to "the best, most reliable instrument available for high-stakes evaluation of teaching" (Teachscape, 2011, p. 1).

For the purposes of our discussion, the implementation of a common metric for evaluating teaching performance opens an avenue not only for capturing these "big data" but also for assigning value to these performances. To date, private software companies already offer (and have studied the application of) badging applications for teacher professional development (Jennings, 2017) and digital competencies (Poldoja, Valjataga, Laanpere, & Tammets, 2014). Such badging software can now be applied to the metric outcomes of teaching evaluation via the Danielson Framework rubrics.

Using the Danielson Framework (or some other nationally recognized set of teacher performance standards), teacher candidates can theoretically be awarded badges for proficiency in planning, instruction, assessment, and professionalism. Such badges would signal to school administrators which candidates are best to hire. These badges would also raise ethical issues for teacher preparation programs regarding the extent to which they would want to graduate candidates who were not proficient in some or all of these standards.

To be clear, such a badging future would still need (at least for now) the presence of human observers to provide the teaching observation scores. When Hans Poldoja and his colleagues (2014) explored ways to assess teachers' digital competencies using DigiMina, they had to rely on humans to peer-evaluate the "higher competency-based tasks" (p. 262). Teaching would clearly qualify under their terms. However, since the observation tool is already completed via human observation, the task of badging would be simple. Given some defined metric (e.g., a mean score of 3 per domain), a teacher might get a "planning badge" or an "assessment badge," certifying his or her competencies in a particular domain.

These badges, as discrete symbols of performance, would create a digital shorthand for teaching effectiveness, creating a de facto merit system using a subjective measure. We know from other social science research that the more a symbol is disassociated from a practice/action, the more the symbol is valued over the spirit of the action. In other words, a person's extrinsic motivation to get the badge by whatever means could outweigh the intrinsic motivation to do well in the task that the symbol represents (in this case, good teaching). It is possible, then, that a teacher would teach a certain way to get a badge rather than alter plans to address a true student need.

Assessing Teacher Performance in Artificial Intelligence Settings

We know it is difficult to get an objective, standardized measurement of teacher performance because the students making up each class, and the characteristics of the class and school as a whole, are so unique. But what if the students weren't real? Would that make a difference? These are questions that the field will have to answer as virtual teaching laboratories become popular measures of teacher performance. For the past two decades, artificial intelligence (AI) researchers have investigated the ways in which pre- and in-service teachers could practice providing instruction in simulated environments. The general idea is not new; many teacher education professors have their students practice lessons in class while their pre-service colleagues pretend to be K–12 students. Artificial intelligence, though, presents the opportunity for virtual students to mirror the thinking and behavior of real-aged students, providing a more authentic simulated experience (Dieker, Hughes, Hynes, & Straub, 2017).

Recent studies have explored the use of simulated classroom environments for both in-service and pre-service teachers. These studies demonstrate not only that these experiences increase the pedagogical knowledge of both those participating in the simulation and those observing it (Ely, Alves,

Dolenc, Sebolt, & Walton, 2018) but also that the duration of the experience does not need to be very long. In a study out of the University of Central Florida, Lisa Dieker and her colleagues (2017) found that just four ten-minute sessions of experience were enough time to increase math teachers' use of focus instructional strategies. Given the hours-long professional development sessions that teachers often sit through, the time-reward ratio of the simulated environment is impressive.

There is currently a race to develop such environments, and funding is available for product development. In fact, two important funders will sound familiar. The TLE TeachLivE (n.d.) simulator was constructed at the University of Central Florida, but funding for the study of its effects of teacher learning comes from the Bill & Melinda Gates Foundation; the project received a $1.5 million grant for research on the simulator (Ferrante, n.d.). Like the MET, this project uses the Danielson Framework for Teaching to assess teacher quality in the simulations.

ETS, the company that supports the SATs, is also developing a simulator to support teacher pedagogical learning (Mikeska, Howell, & Straub, 2019). Like the TLE simulator, ETS is exploring the ways that teachers lead instructional discussions. Avatars serve as the students, behaving in very life-like ways. In fact, the avatars can be directed to discuss among themselves in small groups and then directed back to whole-group discussions. This project is funded by the National Science Foundation and uses a program-developed scoring rubric.

In these simulated environments, teachers are recorded, and their instruction is analyzed via the given rubrics. In some ways, these standardized environments allow for more valid and reliable measures of teacher performance. The contextual factors of a live classroom are mediated, and the teacher can focus on the content and strategy components of instruction without "the problems" of live-student interactions (e.g., bathroom requests, administrator announcements, broken pencils, etc.). These simulated environments can be good training for pre-service teachers and teacher professional development.

It would be wise for us to consider, though, that these programs (and others like them) need funding. The market share of pre-service teachers and teachers engaging in professional development is small. For each, the program marketers would need to convince a university school of education or a school district that the benefits of the simulated environment are worth the cost. The real market share is in mandated use—like requiring all pre-service teachers to use the simulator as part of their certification process. It is at that point that the exploration into whether a good facsimile of a classroom is really good enough to assess teacher learning and performance in a live-classroom environment will become critical.

Teaching in a Changing Landscape

Whether any or all of these changes in teacher performance assessment are truly on the horizon remains to be seen. What we do know is that the field is learning more about how students and teachers learn, how to assess instruction, and how to use technology to observe the most direct measure of teaching—the actual instruction that teachers provide in their classes. The edTPA is born of these developments, as will be future iterations of teacher performance assessments.

Among these potential changes, though, are some maxims of teaching that shouldn't be quickly forgotten. The work that teachers do and the dedication they have for their students is one of the biggest factors of student success (Hattie, 2011). Creating inclusive, supportive instructional environments that challenge students to think ever more deeply about their own thinking and the ways that they communicate their under-standing is critical to good education. In the end, teacher performance assessments will assess the ways in which we engage in those behaviors, but it is in the ways that we genuinely connect with our students that we have the opportunity to make learning come alive for them.

Summary

Technology in the classroom is clearly changing the nature of instruction and assessment. Students continually need to refine digital skills and collaborate in new ways that are more consistent with true twenty-first-century learning. Teachers today, therefore, need an entirely different skill set than the generations of teachers who came before them had. As classroom practices and district curricula continue to evolve to reflect these changes, teacher performance assessments will also need to keep pace with the changes. The future of teacher performance assessments may not yet be known, but it would be prudent to pay attention to changes in your field and seek professional development opportunities that will allow you to continue to grow and evolve as an educator.

ORIENTATION
Where Are You Now?

1 How is technology changing the field of education?

2 What are some ways in which you can keep your own pedagogical skills current throughout your teaching career?

Appendix A

Lesson Plan Template*

Candidate's Name: Class:

Date: Cooperating Teacher:

Lesson Title: Time/Period:

Central Focus. List the central focus for this lesson. Then briefly describe the content of the lesson. This section should respond to the questions, "What am I trying to teach the students?" and "How does this lesson support student learning toward the learning-segment summative assessment?" Also include why this particular lesson is important to teach.

Learning Standards. List the standards *with* the descriptions. Include Common Core and/or appropriate state standards. You should only have one or two standards per lesson.

---

* As noted in chapter 2, the edTPA does not require any specific lesson-planning format. This is just an example of what you might include in your lesson plans. Be sure to follow the guidance of your teacher preparation program.

Lesson Objectives. Each lesson should have a *maximum* of three learning objectives with a *minimum* of two higher-order thinking skills according to Bloom's taxonomy. The objectives should clearly expand on the learning-segment objectives.

Lesson Introduction / Do Now. This initiatory activity should arouse curiosity, connect to prior knowledge, and focus attention on what is to be learned.

Learning Activities. Clearly describe the strategies and procedures that will be employed to achieve the instructional objectives. Strategies incorporate questions, statements, directions, actions, and the sequence in which they occur. Strategies also deal with how the teacher plans to structure and present new subject matter and relate it to the students' prior knowledge. They also indicate teacher and student roles in the lesson. *This should be detailed enough so that any teacher could read the steps to implement the lesson.*

Lesson Closures, Transitions, and Follow-Ups. There should be smooth transitions between activities within each lesson, and each lesson should have a summary activity. Assessments should help guide follow-up activities.

Resources. Provide a comprehensive *list* of all necessary materials including technology, print and nonprint resources, and any other items.

Assessment. Within the learning segment, you must integrate at least two formative assessments and one summative (end-of-the-segment) assessment. Further, specify how you will know that each lesson objective was achieved. Think creatively about evaluation and make sure that the assessment process parallels the emphasis of the lesson (i.e., if your lesson focused on higher-order activities, the evaluation also should emphasize critical thinking). This shift between lessons also might provide opportunities for students to apply, extend, or experiment with what they have learned *and* scaffold students' skills toward the summative (end-of-the-learning-segment) assessment. Provide specific examples of your assessment process—*think rubric!*

References. Using APA citation style, list all references that were used in the development of your lesson, including software, websites, and print and nonprint sources.

Appendix B

Learning Segment Template

Teacher Candidate's Name:

Grade Level/Subject:

Unit Title:

- Learning Segment Title:
  - Lesson 1 Title:
  - Lesson 2 Title:
  - Lesson 3 Title:
  - Lesson 4 Title:
  - Lesson 5 Title:

Central Focus of Learning Segment:

Academic Standard(s) Addressed:

Summative Assessment:

Language Function:

Key Learning Task That Allows Student to Practice Language
Function:

Additional Language Demands:

Identified Language Demands	Planned Language Supports
Vocabulary:	
Syntax:	
Discourse:	

Support for Students' Varied Learning Needs

- Advanced students:

- Students with IEP/504 plans:

- ESL/ELL students:

- Struggling students:

Materials / Use of Instructional Technology:

Instructional Strategies/Activities:

Day 1 Objective: Procedures: Formative Assessment(s):
Day 2 Objective: Procedures: Formative Assessment(s):
Day 3 Objective: Procedures: Formative Assessment(s):
Day 4 Objective: Procedures: Formative Assessment(s):
Day 5 Objective: Procedures: Formative Assessment(s):

References

Apple, M. W. (1996). *Cultural politics and education*. New York: Teachers College Press.

Apple, M. W. (2000). *Official knowledge: Democratic education in a conservative age: Vol. Second Edition*. New York: Routledge.

Aubrey, K., & Riley, A. (2019). *Understanding and using educational theories* (2nd ed.). Newbury Park, CA: Sage.

Bain, K. (2004). *What the best college teachers do*. Cambridge, MA: Harvard University Press.

Banks, J. A., & Banks, C. A. M. (2010). *Multicultural education: Issues and perspectives* (7th ed.). New York: Wiley.

Beck, I. L., McKeown, M. G., & Kucan, L. (2013). *Bringing words to life: Robust vocabulary instruction* (2nd ed.). New York: Guilford.

Bernstein, B. (1996). *Pedagogy, symbolic control and identity: Theory, research, critique*. London: Routledge & Kegan Paul.

Biemans, H. J. A., & Simons, P. R. J. (1996). CONTACT-2: A computer-assisted instructional strategy for promoting conceptual change. *Instructional Science, 24*, 157–176.

Bill & Melinda Gates Foundation. (n.d.). *Measures of Effective Teaching (MET) project*. https://k12education.gatesfoundation.org/blog/measures-of-effective-teaching-met-project/.

Black, P., & Wiliam, D. (1998). Inside the black box: Raising standards through classroom assessment. *Phi Delta Kappan, 80*(2), 139(9).

Black, P., & Wiliam, D. (2009). Developing the theory of formative assessment. *Educational Assessment, Evaluation and Accountability, 21*(1), 5–31. http://dx.doi.org/10.1007/s11092-008-9068-5

Bloom, B. S. (1956). *Taxonomy of educational objectives: The classification of educational goals, Handbook 1: Cognitive Domain.* London: Longmans, Green.

Borden, A. M., Preskill, S. L., & DeMoss, K. (2012). A new turn toward learning for leadership: Findings from an exploratory coursework pilot project. *Journal of Research on Leadership Education, 7*(1), 123–153.

Bower, J., & Thomas, P. L. (Eds.). (2013). *De-testing and de-grading schools: Authentic alternatives to accountability and standardization.* New York: Peter Lang.

Brooks, C., & Young, S. (2011). Are choice-making opportunities needed in the classroom? Using self-determination theory to consider student motivation and learner empowerment. *International Journal of Teaching and Learning in Higher Education, 23*, 48–59.

Bruner, J. (1973). *The relevance of education.* New York: Norton.

Bruner, J. (1986). *Actual minds, possible worlds.* Cambridge, MA: Harvard University Press.

Cannell, J. J. (1987). *Nationally normed elementary achievement testing in America's public schools: How all 50 states are above the national average* (2nd ed.). Daniels, WV: Friends of Education.

Charney, R. S. (2002). *Teaching children to care: Classroom management for ethical and academic growth, K–8.* Turners Falls, MA: Northeast Foundation for Children.

Christie, F., & Martin, J. R. (2007). *Language, knowledge and pedagogy: Functional linguistic and sociological perspectives.* New York: Continuum.

Christie, F., & Maton, K. (Eds.). (2011). *Disciplinarity: Functional linguistic and sociological perspectives.* New York: Continuum.

http://www.bloomsbury.com/us/disciplinarity-functional
-linguistic-and-sociological-perspectives-9781441131805/.

Clayton, C. (2017). Raising the stakes: Objectifying teaching
in the edTPA and Danielson rubrics. In J. H. Carter & H. A.
Lochte (Eds.), *Teacher performance assessment and accountability reforms: The impacts of edTPA on teaching and schools* (pp.
79–105). New York: Palgrave Macmillan.

Cochran-Smith, M., Carney, M. C., Keefe, E. S., Burton, S., Chang,
W.-C., Fernandez, M. B., Miller, A. F., Sanchez, J. G., & Baker,
M. (2018). *Reclaiming accountability in teacher education*. New
York: Teachers College Press.

Coffin, C. (2006). *Historical discourse: The language of time, cause
and evaluation* (K. Hyland, Ed.). New York: Continuum.

Covey, S. (2004). *The 7 habits of highly effective people: Powerful
lessons in personal change*. New York: Simon & Schuster.

Croddy, M., & Levine, P. (2014). The C3 framework: A powerful
tool for preparing future generations for informed and engaged
civic life. *Social Education, 78*(6), 282–285.

Culatta, R. (2020). Constructivist theory (Jerome Bruner). *Instruc-
tionalDesign.org*. http://www.instructionaldesign.org/theories/
constructivist/.

Darling-Hammond, L. (2017). *Developing and measuring higher
order skills: Models for state performance assessment systems*.
Learning Policy Institute and Council of Chief State School
Officers, Palo Alto, CA.

de Bruin, L. R. (2019). The use of cognitive apprenticeship in the
learning and teaching of improvisation: Teacher and student
perspectives. *Research Studies in Music Education, 41*(3), 261–279.

Decker, G. (2015, July 9). New York ditches controversial test-
maker Pearson. *Chalkbeat.org*. https://chalkbeat.org/posts/
ny/2015/07/09/new-york-ditches-controversial-test-maker
-pearson/.

De Graaff, E., & Kolmos, A. (2003). Characteristics of problem-based learning. *International Journal of Engineering Education*, 19(5), 657–662.

De La Paz, S., Monte-Sano, C., Felton, M., Croninger, R., Jackson, C., & Piantedosi, K. W. (2016). A historical writing apprenticeship for adolescents: Integrating disciplinary learning with cognitive strategies. *Reading Research Quarterly*, 52(1), 31–52.

Delisle, R. (1997). *How to use problem-based learning in the classroom*. Alexandria, VA: Association for Supervision and Curriculum Development.

DeMoss, K. (2017). New York's edTPA: The perfect solution to a wrongly identified problem. In J. H. Carter & H. A. Lochte (Eds.), *Teacher performance assessment and accountability reforms: The impacts of edTPA on teaching and schools* (pp. 25–46). New York: Palgrave Macmillan.

Dewey, J. (1916). *Democracy and education*. New York: Free Press.

Dewey, J. (1938). *Experience and education: Vol. 60th anniversary edition*. Indianapolis: Kappa Delta Pi.

Dieker, L. A., Hughes, C. E., Hynes, M. C., & Straub, C. (2017). Using simulated virtual environments to improve teacher performance. *School-University Partnership*, 10(3), 62–81.

Ding, M., Li, X., Piccolo, D., & Kulm, G. (2007) Teacher interventions in cooperative-learning mathematics classes. *Journal of Educational Research*, 100(3), 162–175.

Dweck, C. S. (1999). *Self-theories: Their role in motivation, personality and development*. London: Taylor and Francis / Psychology Press.

Dweck, C. S. (2006). *Mindset: The new psychology of success*. New York: Random House.

Ely, E., Alves, K. D., Dolenc, N. R., Sebolt, S., & Walton, E. A. (2018). Classroom simulation to prepare teachers to use evidence-based comprehension practices. *Journal of Digital Learning in Teacher Education*, 34(2), 71–87.

Eyal, L. (2012). Digital assessment literacy: The core role of the teacher in a digital environment. *Educational Technology & Society, 15*(2), 37–49.

Fang, Z., & Schleppegrell, M. (2010). Disciplinary literacies across content areas: Supporting secondary reading through functional language analysis. *Journal of Adolescent & Adult Literacy, 53*(7), 587–597.

Fantaneanu, T. A., Bhattacharyya, S., Milligan, T., & Pennell, P. B. (2016). Rapidly cycling auras and episodic focal dystonia in anti-LGI1 autoimmune encephalitis. *JAMA Neurology, 73*(9), 1150.

Ferrante, D. (n.d.). Kickin' it new school: A cutting-edge classroom simulator at UCF is helping educators become better teachers. *Pegasus: The Magazine of the University of Central Florida.* https://www.ucf.edu/pegasus/kickin-new-school/.

FitzGerald, F. (1979). *America revised.* New York: Little, Brown.

Fitzgerald, J. C. (2012). "It doesn't say": Exploring students' understandings of asyndetic constructions in history textbooks. *Social Studies Research and Practice, 7*(3).

Fosnot, C. T. (2005). *Constructivism: Theory, perspectives, and practice.* New York: Teachers College Press.

Fredrick, T. A. (2008). Facilitating better teamwork: Analyzing the challenges and strategies of classroom-based collaboration. *Business Communication Quarterly, 71*(4), 439–455.

Freire, P. (1970). *Pedagogy of the oppressed.* New York: Continuum.

Frisby, B. N., & Martin, M. M. (2010). Instructor-student and student-student rapport in the classroom. *Communication Education, 2*, 146–164.

Gallagher, K. (2009). *Readicide: How schools are killing reading and what you can do about it.* Portsmouth, NH: Stenhouse.

Gay, G. (2000). *Culturally responsive teaching: Theory, research, and practice.* New York: Teachers College Press.

Giroux, H. A. (1995). Language, difference and curriculum theory: Beyond the politics of clarity. In P. L. McLaren & J. M. Giarelli

(Eds.), *Critical theory and educational research*. Albany: State University of New York Press.

Grant, A. (2016). *Originals: How non-conformists move the world*. New York: Penguin Random House.

Halliday, M. A. K., & Matthiessen, C. M. I. M. (2004). *An introduction to functional grammar* (Vol. 3). London: Hodder Education.

Hansen, L. (2013). 8 drivers who blindly followed their GPS into disaster. *The Week*. https://theweek.com/articles/464674/8-drivers-who-blindly-followed-gps-into-disaster

Hargreaves, A., & Fullan, M. (2012). *Professional capital: Transforming teaching in every school*. New York: Teachers College Press.

Hattie, J. (2011). *Visible learning for teachers: Maximizing impact on learning*. New York: Routledge.

Heath, S. B. (1983). *Ways with words: Language, life and work in communities and classrooms*. Cambridge: Cambridge University Press.

Hollie, S. (2018). *Culturally and linguistically responsive teaching and learning*. Huntington Beach, CA: Shell Education.

Honore, C. (2013). *The slow fix: Solve problems, work smarter, and live better*. New York: HarperCollins.

Humphrey, S. (2017). *Academic literacies in the middle years*. New York: Routledge.

Jennings, J. (2017, July). The future-ready teachers badge group [Educational]. *AdvancingK12*. https://www.skyward.com/discover/blog/skyward-blogs/skyward-executive-blog/july-2017/badges-for-future-ready-teachers.

Johnson, A. G. (2005). *Privilege, power, and difference* (2nd ed.). New York: McGraw-Hill.

Kaarakainen, M.-T., Kivinen, O., & Vainio, T. (2018). Performance-based testing for ICT skills assessing: A case study of students and teachers' ICT skills in Finnish schools. *Universal Access in the Information Society, 17*, 349–360.

Kintsch, W. (1998). *Comprehension: A paradigm for cognition.* Cambridge: Cambridge University Press.

Kohler, F. W., Henning, J. E., & Usma-Wilches, J. (2008). Preparing preservice teachers to make instructional decisions: An examination of data from the teacher work sample. *Teaching and Teacher Education, 24*(8), 2108–2117.

Koretz, D. (1988). Arriving at Lake Wobegon: Are standardized tests exaggerating achievement and distorting instruction? *American Educator, 12*(2), 8–15, 46–52.

Krathwohl, D. R. (2002). A revision of Bloom's taxonomy: An overview. *Theory into Practice, 41*(4), 212–218.

Krishnan, A. (2009). *What are academic disciplines? Some observations on the disciplinarity vs. Interdisciplinarity debate.* Southampton, UK: ESRC National Centre for Research Methods. http://eprints.ncrm.ac.uk/783/1/what_are_academic _disciplines.pdf.

Kulasegaram, K., & Rangachari, P. K. (2018). Beyond "formative": Assessments to enrich student learning. *Advances in Physiology Education, 42*, 5–14.

Labaree, D. F. (2010). *Someone has to fail: The zero-sum game of public schooling.* Cambridge, MA: Harvard University Press.

Larsson, P. N. (2018). "We're talking about mobility": Discourse strategies for promoting disciplinary knowledge and language in educational contexts. *Linguistics and Education, 48*, 61–75.

Leikin, R., & Zaslavsky, O. (1997). Facilitating student interactions in mathematics in a cooperative learning setting. *Journal for Research in Mathematics Education, 28*(3), 331–354.

Leinhardt, G. (2010). Introduction: Explaining instructional explanations. In M. K. Stein & L. Kucan (Eds.), *Instructional explanations in the disciplines* (pp. 1–5). New York: Springer.

Linn, R. L. (1994, November 7). *Assessment-based reform: Challenges to educational measurement.* The first annual William H. Angoff Memorial Lecture, Princeton, NJ.

Lortie, D. C. (1975). *Schoolteacher: A sociological study*. Chicago: University of Chicago Press.

Martin, J. R. (1989). Technicality and abstraction: Language for the creation of specialized texts. In F. Christie (Ed.), *Writing in schools* (pp. 36–44). Melbourne: Deakin University Press.

Maton, K., Hood, S., & Shay, S. (Eds.). (2017). *Knowledge-building: Educational studies in legitimation code theory*. New York: Routledge.

Meyer, A., Rose, D. H., & Gordon, D. (2016). *Universal design for learning: Theory and practice*. Wakefield, MA: CAST Professional.

Mikeska, J. N., Howell, H., & Straub, C. (2019). Using performance tasks within simulated environments to assess teachers' ability to engage in coordinated, accumulated, and dynamic (CAD) competencies. *International Journal of Testing, 19*(2), 128–147. https://doi.org/10.1080/15305058.2018.1551223.

Montessori, M. (1965). *Spontaneous activity in education*. New York: Schocken.

Moon, E. C. (2018). Teaching students out of harm's way: Mitigating digital knowledge gaps and digital risk created by 1:1 device programs in K–12 education in the USA. *Journal of Information, Communication and Ethics in Society, 16*(3), 290–302.

National Research Council (2013). *Next generation science standards: For states, by states*. Washington, DC: National Academies Press.

Newmann, F. M. (1992). *Student engagement and achievement in American secondary schools*. New York: Teachers College Press.

Newport, C. (2016). *Deep work: Rules for focused success in a distracted world*. New York: Grand Central.

Noddings, N. (2013). *Education and democracy in the 21st century*. New York: Teachers College Press.

November, A. (2012). *Who owns the learning? Preparing students for success in the digital age*. Bloomington, IN: Solution Tree.

Ottesen, E. (2007). Reflection in teacher education. *Reflective Practice, 8*(1), 31–46.

Oxford Reference. (n.d.). *Lake Wobegon effect*. Retrieved November 12, 2020, from https://www.oxfordreference.com/view/10.1093/oi/authority.20110810105237549.

Palmer, P. J. (2007). *The courage to teach: Exploring the inner landscape of a teacher's life*. New York: Wiley.

Parkay, F. W. (2016). *Becoming a teacher* (10th ed.). London: Pearson.

Pecheone, R. L., & Whittaker, A. (2016). Well-prepared teachers inspire student learning. *Phi Delta Kappan, 97*(7), 8–13.

Perkins, D. (1999). The many faces of constructivism. *Educational Leadership, 57*(3), 6–11.

Pinsker, J. (2015, March). People who use Firefox or Chrome are better employees. *The Atlantic*. https://www.theatlantic.com/business/archive/2015/03/people-who-use-firefox-or-chrome-are-better-employees/387781/

Polakow-Suransky, S., Thomases, J., & DeMoss, K. (2016, July 8). Train teachers like doctors. *New York Times* (Online).

Poldoja, H., Valjataga, T., Laanpere, M., & Tammets, K. (2014). Web-based self- and peer-assessment of teachers' digital competencies. *World Wide Web, 17*, 255–269.

Ravitch, D. (2014). *Reign of error: The hoax of the privatization movement and the danger to America's public schools* (Reprint ed.). New York: Vintage.

Ravitch, D. (2016). *The death and life of the great American school system: How testing and choice are undermining education*. New York: Basic Books.

Reyna, J., & Meier, P. (2018). Using the learner-generated digital media (LGDM) framework in tertiary science education: A pilot study. *Education Sciences, 8*(106).

Robinson, K. (2011). *Out of our minds: Learning to be creative* (2nd ed.). Chichester, UK: Capstone.

Rodriguez, V., & Fitzpatrick, M. (2014). *The teaching brain: An evolutionary trait at the heart of education.* New York: New Press.

Rose, D., & Martin, J. R. (2012). *Learning to write, reading to learn: Genre, knowledge and pedagogy in the Sydney School.* Sheffield, UK: Equinox.

Rose, T. (2015). *The end of average: How we succeed in a world that values sameness.* New York: Harper One.

Ryan, R. M., & Deci, E. L. (2000). Self-determination theory and the facilitation of intrinsic motivation, social development, and well-being. *American Psychologist, 55*(1), 68–78.

Sadler, D. R. (1998). Formative assessment: Revisiting the territory. *Assessment in Education: Principles, Policy & Practice, 5*(1), 77–84.

Sahlberg, P. (2014). *Finnish lessons 2.0: What can the world learn from educational change in Finland?* (2nd ed.). New York: Teachers College Press.

Sato, M. (2014). What is the underlying conception of teaching of the edTPA? *Journal of Teacher Education, 65*(5), 421–434.

Schalock, D., & Schalock, M. (2011). Teacher work sample methodology at Western Oregon University. In H. Rosselli, M. Girod, & M. Brodsky (Eds.), *Connecting teaching and learning: History, evolution, and case studies of teacher work sample methodology* (pp. 1–24). Lanham, MD: Rowman & Littlefield.

Schleppegrell, M. (2004). *The language of schooling: A functional linguistics perspective.* Mahwah, NJ: Lawrence Erlbaum.

Schneider, J. (2011). *Excellence for all: How a new breed of reformers is transforming America's public schools.* Nashville, TN: Vanderbilt University Press.

Shanahan, T., & Shanahan, C. (2008). Teaching disciplinary literacy to adolescents: Rethinking content-area literacy. *Harvard Educational Review, 78*(1), 40–59.

Shulman, L. S. (1986). Those who understand: Knowledge growth in teaching. *Educational Researcher, 15*(2), 4–14.

Simonsen, B., Fairbanks, S., Briesch, A., Myers, D., & Sugai, G.

(2008). Evidence-based practices in classroom management. *Education and Treatment of Children, 31*(3), 351–380.

Singer, N. (2017, May 13). How Google took over the classroom. *New York Times.* https://www.nytimes.com/2017/05/13/technology/google-education-chromebooks-schools.html.

Spiller, P. (2017, May 29). Could subjects soon be a thing of the past in Finland? *BBC.* https://www.bbc.com/news/world-europe-39889523.

Stanford Center for Assessment, Learning, and Equity (SCALE). (2016). *Secondary history / social studies assessment handbook.* Palo Alto, CA: Board of Trustees of the Leland Stanford Junior University.

Strauss, V. (2018, July 17). How the Gates Foundation could have saved itself and taxpayers more than half a billion dollars. *Washington Post.* https://www.washingtonpost.com/news/answer-sheet/wp/2018/07/17/how-the-gates-foundation-could-have-saved-itself-and-taxpayers-more-than-half-a-billion-dollars/.

Taylor, H. (2015, December 9). Google's Chromebooks make up half of US classroom devices sold. *CNBC.* https://www.cnbc.com/2015/12/03/googles-chromebooks-make-up-half-of-us-classroom-devices.html.

Teachscape. (2011). *Teachscape Proposal: Appendix A: The Framework for Teaching (2011 Revised Edition).* https://usny.nysed.gov/rttt/teachers-leaders/practicerubrics/Docs/Teachscape_Rubric.pdf.

TLE TeachLivE. (n.d.). *About CREST/TeachLivE.* Retrieved November 12, 2020, http://teachlive.org/about/about-teachlive/.

Valenzuela, A. (1999). *Subtractive schooling: U.S.-Mexican youth and the politics of caring.* Albany: State University of New York Press.

Vygotsky, L. S. (1978). *Mind in society: The development of higher psychological processes* (Vol. 14). Cambridge, MA: Harvard University Press.

Wagner, T. (2008). *The global achievement gap: Why even our best schools don't teach the new survival skills our children need—And what we can do about it.* New York: Basic Books.

Wagner, T. (2012). *Creating innovators: The making of young people who will change the world.* New York: Scribner.

Walker, T. (2016, August 29). What's the purpose of education? Public doesn't agree on the answer. *NEA Today.* http://neatoday .org/2016/08/29/the-purpose-of-education-pdk-poll/.

West Sider. (2013, May 1). GPS, brain fail driver: Car ends up stuck on Riverside Park stairs. *West Side Rag.* https://www.westsiderag .com/2013/05/01/gps-brain-fail-driver-car-ends-up-stuck-on -riverside-park-stairs.

Wiggins, G. J., & McTighe, J. (2005). *Understanding by design* (2nd ed.). London: Pearson.

Wineburg, S. (2001). *Historical thinking and other unnatural acts.* Philadelphia: Temple University Press.

Wineburg, S. (2018). *Why learn history when it's already on your phone.* Chicago: University of Chicago Press.

Woolfolk, A. (2007). *Educational psychology* (10th ed.). Boston: Allyn and Bacon.

World Economic Forum. (2017). *Mitigating risks in the innovation economy.* http://www.weforum.org/whitepapers/mitigating -risks-in-the-innovation-economy.

Zvauya, R., Purandare, S., Young, N., & Pallan, M. (2017) The use of mind maps as an assessment tool in a problem based learning course. *Creative Education, 8,* 1782–1793. doi: 10.4236/ ce.2017.811122.

Zwiers, J. (2008). *Building academic language: Essential practices for content classrooms.* San Francisco: Jossey-Bass.

Zwiers, J. (2014). *Building academic language: Meeting Common Core standards across disciplines, grades 5–12.* San Francisco: Jossey-Bass.

Index

abstract representations, in constructivism, 68

academic language: content communication in, 83; as disciplinary-specific, 84–85, 106–107; discourse in, 97–100; edTPA and, 83–84, 85; edTPA student use of, 105, 106; edTPA symbol use in, 92; language function, 85–91; "language of schooling" differentiation in, 84; planning supports, 101–103; research reliance in, 91; sentence framing in, 103–104; syntax tied to, 93–97; text importance and learning curve in, 108; vocabulary in, 91–93; Wineburg and reliability of sources, 107

academic learning, prior, 68, 69, 82, 148; assessments of, 72, 73, 74; continuous student communication in, 74–75; curriculum information gathering, 73; Kintsch's comprehension model, 70–71; subway map exercise, 71–72; teacher use of, 75

academic vocabulary, 91–93; general academic terms, 92–93; research reliance in, 91; social language meanings, 92; vocabulary-rich environments creation in, 91–92

accredited programs, 20–21

American Council on the Teaching of Foreign Languages (ACTFL), 149

analysis, strategies for, 143–145, 148

anonymous peer evaluations, 124

artificial intelligence (AI) settings: avatar use in, 173; ETS development in, 173; live-student interaction mediated in, 173–174; teacher performance assessment in, 172–174; virtual teaching laboratories, popularity in, 172

assessment: analysis, 148, 152, 160; levels of, 34–35. *See also under specific assessments*

assessment data, 14, 45, 53, 134, 152; of AI on teacher performance, 172–174; compliance view of, 24, 26; constant reflection in, 133; daily routines, 140–141; edTPA driven by, 15, 155; feedback direct and specific in, 135; of PBL, 59–60; of prior academic learning, 72, 73, 74; student learning in, 133, 134, 135–143; teacher effectiveness analysis in, 143–151; teacher technology and, 161; teaching practices and instructional decisions, reflection in, 133

assessment planning: data gathering in, 45; development ideas for, 153–154; formative assessments in, 45–52, 62; instruction design and,

About the Authors

Jason C. Fitzgerald, PhD, is a faculty member at Monmouth University, where he teaches secondary social studies education and educational leadership courses. Formerly, he served as a professor-in-residence, teaching and mentoring candidates and early-career teachers inside the school context. He has taught about the edTPA since 2012 at two universities.

Michelle L. Schpakow, EdD, is a faculty member in the Department of Curriculum and Instruction at Monmouth University. She serves on the university's edTPA implementation committee and assists with the mentorship and supervision of student teachers. She also works for Pearson Education, Inc., as an edTPA scorer.